Clos[ ] Closet

Testimonies of Deliverance From Homosexuality

Talbert W. Swan, II
Editor

Trumpet in Zion Publishing
Indian Orchard, MA

Trumpet in Zion Publishing
www.tzpublishing.com

Library of Congress Control Number: 2002096386

ISBN 0-9716355-2-8

DEDICATION

To the thousands of men and women who have either overcome or are in the process of overcoming the homosexual lifestyle. May the peace of the Consolator be your portion.

"And such were some of you. But you were washed, you were sanctified, you were justified in the name of the Lord Jesus Christ and by the Spirit of our God." (1 Corinthians 6:11)

CONTENTS

ACKNOWLEDGMENTS

I thank my family for being loving, understanding, supportive and for being by my side through all the trials and tribulations of life.

A special thanks goes to my administrative assistant, Leslie Smith for assisting me in bringing together the wonderful individuals who have contributed to this book.

It was a blessing to have Pastor D.L. Foster and Dr. John R. Diggs, Jr. write the *foreword* and the *afterword* respectively. These two men have greatly inspired me. I thank God for their friendship.

Many special thanks to the members, staff, and leadership of the Solid Rock Church of God in Christ for your patience, inspiration, and encouragement. Thank you for allowing me to serve as your pastor.

Most of all, I thank Almighty God for granting me favor, love, grace, and mercy. Without you I could do nothing.

PREFACE

When we testify of the power of God in the presence of people, the weak gain strength, the sick receive hope, and the grieved are comforted. Christians are the witnesses that Almighty God performs great works in the lives of His people. Therefore, we have an obligation to speak of God's goodness, His delivering power and His grace and mercy. Our testimonies present evidence that God is a healer, a comforter and a deliverer.

Of course, whenever we become witnesses, we encounter those who attempt to discredit our testimony. As America has become more and more accepting of the homosexual lifestyle, it has given rise to those who are determined to vilify anyone who dares testify that, "God delivered me from homosexuality." Deliverance from homosexuality has been termed as the "ex-gay myth" by homosexual activists in their attempt to deny the power of an All Powerful God in exchange for political correctness. The gay lobby has used God as a scapegoat to justify sinful behavior. After all, if homosexuality is an immutable trait like eye color or left-handedness, how could God be so cynical to "make" people gay and then condemn their lifestyle as an abomination?

When the Massachusetts Supreme Judicial Court ruled in November 2003 that it was illegal to ban same-sex marriage it renewed the debate on homosexuality across America. Arguments over whether or not homosexuality is genetic raged over the television and radio airwaves and in the print media. How to interpret biblical references concerning homosexuality was also a hot topic. I found myself in the midst of many of these debates during my weekly radio broadcast, at rallies, forums, on the evening news and in newspaper articles on the subject. Often it seemed as though I was hitting my head against a brick wall as I advocated for traditional marriage and repudiated the invalid comparison of the gay lobby's fight to legalize same-sex marriage with the civil rights movement. Many of the responses I received from supporters of the homosexual agenda confirmed how far the homosexualization of America has come. Today, those who dare oppose same sex marriage or speak against the sin of homosexuality are looked upon as being "closed-minded," hateful and bigoted.

In spite of the many hateful letters, telephone calls, and emails I have received as a direct result of my opposition to gay marriage, I continue to hold fast to a position that is supported by the Word of God. Marriage is a God-ordained institution that does not exist simply for the emotional satisfaction of two individuals. Marriage exists for the greater good of the entire society and stands under the blessing or curse of God. From the beginning of time marriage has been established as a union between male and female. The legalization of same-sex marriage is an attempt to put misguided emotional fulfillment before right actions and God-given principles. This will only further corrupt an already morally challenged society and further the collapse of the American family. Furthermore, I am convinced that to condone same-sex marriage is to bring about the judgment of God on America. Sin flaunted in the name of progression and enlightenment in order to satisfy the wishes of a vocal, well funded, minority group is a moral travesty that every Christian must stand against.

Sadly, many Christian leaders have bowed to the pressure of homosexual activists and have adopted a fallacious theology that affirms homosexuality as an acceptable lifestyle in the eyes of God. Preachers have become reluctant to preach the truth concerning homosexuality for fear of being labeled as narrow-minded, conservative, or bigoted. Be that as it may, the fear of some to anger the gay lobby doesn't change the fact that the Bible regards homosexuality as unnatural and as an abomination.

"…whenever we become witnesses, we encounter those who attempt to discredit our testimony."

To be clear and to dispel the argument that such an admonition is one based on hatred, let me state for the record that homosexuals are indeed human beings created in the image of God and loved by their Creator. In spite of the sin of homosexuality, the duty of the Christian is to lead the homosexual out of a lifestyle that will end in pain, despair, and eternal damnation. Unfortunately, the media has sensationalized the extreme cases of religious fanatics, who indeed preach a vile message of hatred against the homosexual. This image of religious hatred is an extreme barrier to productive dialogue with the homosexual. Fortunately, this barrier can be broken down by the love of Jesus Christ and through the testimonies of those who have experienced the same vilification and rejection that many gays have, those who have overcome the homosexual lifestyle.

While I believe the argument against same-sex marriage and the homosexual lifestyle is strong, the best argument against the myth of homosexuality as an innate trait is the testimonies of those who have overcome. The one thing that the gay lobby has been ineffective in arguing against is the testimony of deliverance. People may argue over doctrine, science, and correct biblical interpretation, however, they cannot argue about what God has done in the lives of overcomers. This book is a presentation of many testimonies about how God has changed lives through the gospel of truth.

Closing the Closet details the transformation of God's people. Former lifestyles that consisted of homosexual relationships, promiscuity, drug abuse and other addictions have been changed through the awesome power of God. These pages contain the stories of people who were lost until coming into the saving knowledge of Jesus Christ.

Rev. Talbert W. Swan, II, Th.M.
Editor

FOREWORD

Who would have ever imagined that an inconspicuous little room could become the focal point of such a fierce spiritual warfare? Sometimes, it is amazing what we perceive to be insignificant really are monumental markers in human history. Such is the case with "the closet." Before you begin reading this incredible collection of true stories —on the other side of the closet door— let me tell you why this book is necessary.

Over the decades the closet has evolved into the epitomic symbol of darkness and shame. Consequently, the equally evolving homosexual community, masters at the art of redefinition, made it chic to "come out of the closet" as a way of defining their quest for self-imposed freedom. Thousands of homosexuals began pouring out of the dark places they lived in, introducing themselves to a gasping society via one of the most mistrusted sexual lifestyles ever embraced by humanity. Coming out for gays meant freedom. But many discovered that coming out of the closet was a pipe dream, a magnanimous fraud brought on by misguided idealisms and broken visions of people who created their own choices.

Many were led to believe that coming out of the closet was the fast track to happiness and acceptance homosexuals craved, but society was unwilling to fulfill. They thought that it would mean an auto-renewable license to once and for all shed the rigid moral attitudes about sex between people of the same gender and live happily ever after. After all gay meant good, right?

But, the fairy tale of coming out imploded like Cinderella's grand chariot turning back into a pumpkin. Sin promised a lifetime Mardi Gras, but could only deliver perhaps a few years of drug induced highs.

The closet, with all of its protective darkness, for some, is still a symbol of that which is shameful. Coming out of it means more to former homosexuals because closing the door to that closet is the true freedom promised by Jesus' redemptive blood.

We used to sing a powerful song growing up in church. Do you remember it?

Tell me, who's report will you believe? We shall believe the report of the Lord! His report says I am healed, His report says I am filled. His report says I am free, his report says victory!

Thankfully, Pastor Talbert W. Swan, II has sought out and brought together stories of overcoming homosexuality from the people who matter most. These stories are not cunningly devised fables and are entwined within the fabric of the "report of the Lord." I was very excited to be asked to *foreword* this project because I know the pain of living life as a homosexual and I'm a witness to the joyful freedom of coming out of homosexuality, thereby closing the closet door that held me captive for over 11years.

These stories of change and transformation told by former homosexuals must become part of the church's offense against the rising tide of homosexual acceptance. Through ridicule and controversy, our stories have survived to give God the glory and to present a past imperfect model of what happens when homosexuals truly submit themselves to the Lordship of Jesus Christ.

"...the equally evolving homosexual community, masters at the art of redefinition, made it chic to 'come out of the closet'"

It is imperative to encapsulate the stories of former homosexuals for many reasons. A few come to mind: for people who need hope for change in their own lives, as a testament that the power of God is real and vibrant in transforming the homosexual; for the naysayers and doubters; for friends and families of homosexuals; and for church leaders to understand that redemption is a far greater spiritual priority than condemnation.

I count Pastor Swan as a friend, a brother and fellow frontline soldier. First as a co-laborer in the Gospel and secondly as a man who, when confronted with the challenge of homosexual activism, responded with bold courage. He turned the confrontation on its head by doing what every man of God should do: bring out the witnesses to God's power!

If this were a debate about whether someone could get free from years of drug abuse, there's one sure way to resolve it. If we were unsure about whether smokers could stop smoking or prostitutes could stop hooking or if thieves could stop stealing, men and women who have left those vices behind would be called out for testimony. And now, in a nation at the crossroads of indecision about homosexuality, those who have been delivered and set free by the power of God and are healing through the fellowship of the saints need to be brought out into the open. Pastor Swan has done just that with this timely book. Like a football player going after a fumbled ball, he's picked up that challenge and though not having experienced the struggle we have endured, he has encouraged us to take our place in the halls of faith, after we have closed —for good— the closet doors of sin.

As you read, allow yourself room to experience joy, sadness, humor, deep love, shock, excitement, and most of all gratitude for what each writer has been through. Today this book brings a fresh new perspective to the debates over homosexuality. Not only for today, but as we progress towards the coming of our Lord Jesus, our children need a strong record to guide them in their choices. *Closing the Closet* is that investment of truth and reality the church needs in such a time like this.

Pastor Darryl L. Foster
Author, *Touching A Dead Man: One Man's explosive story of deliverance from homosexuality*

Executive Director, Witness! Freedom Ministries, Inc.
Atlanta, GA

1
Can Homosexuals Change?

By

Sue Bohlin

Mike[1]was marching in a Gay Pride parade when God got a hold of him. He had been high for four days and his "buzz" suddenly evaporated as he heard a voice in his head say, "You don't have to live like this." He knew beyond a shadow of a doubt that it was God offering him a way out. He put down his Gay Pride sign, left the parade, sat down in a nearby stairwell, and repented of his rebellion. He gave his heart to Jesus Christ and starting walking out of homosexuality that day. Today, several years later, he is married with a child, and living a very different kind of life. Not just on the outside; his heart was changed from the inside out.

Randy was on a self-destructive path of drug and alcohol abuse and homosexual activity. When he told his mother he was gay, she threw him out of the house, and the only place he could find belonging, safety, and identity was the gay community. As he spent more and more time "escaping" the pain in his life through sex and alcohol, he began to realize how bad his life was. He wanted to die but God had something else in mind.

Randy was invited to a Bible study where he met a man who had left the gay lifestyle and was living a changed life. For the first time he honestly called out and said, "God, please help me."

One of his friends became a Christian. He asked her about homosexuality and was angered by her initial response. She said, "I now believe it is a sin--but God wouldn't call it a sin if there weren't something better." Randy eventually realized that he was a sinner who needed God's love and grace, and in 1992 he trusted Christ as his Savior. Two months later, he was led to Living Hope, an organization that helps people walk out of homosexuality through an intimate relationship with Jesus Christ. He left his homosexual identity behind and embraced his true identity as a child of God, committed to holiness and purity. Randy is now director of that ministry and is helping others walk out of homosexuality. He's not perfect, he's still growing . . . just like me and every other Christian I know. But the "something better" God had in mind for him is an intimacy with Christ that is breathtaking.

Randy brings glory to God every day of his life by living out the abiding truth that change is possible.

Stories of Women

Carol grew up in a religious home with parents whose standards were too strict to allow her to please them. But she was smart, and a good student, and her teachers gave her the affirmation and encouragement her heart longed for. She developed very strong bonds with her teachers, some of which became profound emotional dependencies.

2

In graduate school, she was hit by the unexpected pain of loneliness and emptiness. Carol got into an intense relationship with a married woman, facing completely new temptations. She was totally unprepared to resist the strength of same-gender attraction, and quickly found herself emotionally and physically involved in a relationship she couldn't believe was happening. Now she was not only emotionally needy, she was shackled by deep shame, woundedness, and guilt.

A friend told her about a ministry to those dealing with same-sex attraction, and it was like finding a door to another world. Through the support she found there, Carol was challenged to identify the lies of Satan which she had believed her whole life and replace them with the truth of Scripture. God is renewing her mind, meeting her deep heart-needs, and bringing her to a place of freedom and hope.

Diane's story is different. She spent eighteen years in a committed lesbian relationship with another woman she believed to be her soul-mate. They went through a commitment ceremony in a gay church, and raised a daughter together. She enjoyed a position of leadership as a bright and articulate spokesperson for a gay church.

"...the 'something better' God had in mind for him is an intimacy with Christ that is breathtaking."

Through all those years, Diane's mother was steadfast in three things. She loved Diane unconditionally. She never backed down about her belief that her daughter's lifestyle was sinful because God says it's wrong. And third, she prayed faithfully for her daughter.

Diane and her partner sought the Lord about everything except their sexuality. At one point, they were praying together for wisdom and truth about a situation that had nothing to do with their relationship. God answered their prayer in an unexpected way; He showed them the truth about the sinful nature of their relationship. It was a terribly painful and unwelcome discovery to learn that they had been deceived. Together, they decided out of obedience to God to separate and break off their relationship. It's still painful, even as Diane experiences God's healing touch in the deepest parts of her wounded soul. He's changing Diane and Carol from the inside out.

Three Claims for Change

Some people deal with same-sex attraction by pretending it's not there. Denial is unfortunately the time-honored "Christian" response. But this is not the way God wants us to deal with problems; Psalm 51:6 says, "Surely you desire truth in my inmost parts." Acknowledging one has a homosexual orientation is like seeing the red light on your car's dashboard; it means something is wrong somewhere. A homosexual orientation isn't the actual problem; it's the symptom of a deeper issue-- legitimate, God-given needs for relationship and intimacy that have been channeled in unhealthy and sinful directions.

But it is not a simple matter, and it would be disrespectful to imply that there is an easy solution to the complex issue of homosexuality. Among those who claim that change is possible, there are three main schools of thought on how to get there.

The first is the deliverance ministries. They say that homosexuality is caused by a demon, and if we can just cast out the demon, the problem is gone. Sounds like an easy fix, but it ends up causing even more problems because homosexuality isn't caused by a demon. The person who was "delivered" may experience a temporary emotional high, but the same temptations and thought patterns that plagued him before are going to return because the root issue wasn't dealt with. Only now, he's burdened by the false guilt of thinking he did something wrong or that he's not good enough for God to "fix" him.

A second and more effective treatment for homosexuality is reparative therapy. There is a lot of wisdom to be found here because many therapists believe that homosexuality has its roots in hurtful relationship patterns, especially with family members, and many homosexual men and women report exactly that. But reparative therapy is often just behavior modification, and it deals only with the flesh, that part of us independent of God. Reparative therapy can make people feel better, but it can't bring true inner healing.

The third, and I believe best, way to bring about real and lasting change is a redemptive approach. Ministries that disciple men and women in intimate relationship with Jesus Christ are able to lead them into inner healing because God transforms His people. There are many organizations that provide support and education and discipleship

It's excruciatingly difficult to leave homosexuality without support. Fortunately, even for people who do not live in an area where there is an Exodus referral ministry, there are online support forums that are almost as powerful as face-to-face groups. There are also some wonderful books available, particularly *Coming Out of Homosexuality* by Bob Davies, and

Someone I Love is Gay by Anita Worthen and Bob Davies. Another excellent book is *You Don't Have to Be Gay* by Jeff Konrad. But discipleship is hard work, and there is no simple and easy fix.

The Path to True Change

The most effective route to real, lasting change for those caught in same-gender attraction is a redemptive approach. This means discipleship, being taught and encouraged and held accountable to develop intimacy with Christ. Interestingly, it doesn't seem to matter what the particular stronghold is in a person's life--whether it be homosexuality, gluttony, drug dependency, compulsive gambling or shopping, alcoholism, sexual addiction, or any other stronghold--the most effective solution is the same: intimacy with Christ.

True discipleship is hard work. And God even gives us the energy for discipleship! But it takes tremendous self-discipline to choose to operate in the Spirit instead of in our own flesh, to depend on God's strength instead of our own. The real battle is in the mind. The steps to overcoming homosexuality also apply to overcoming any stronghold.

First, the person has to stop the sinful behavior. It's best to ask for God's help. This is no different from the requirement for any drug or alcohol abuse treatment. You can't work on a problem when you're still totally controlled by it.

The second step is to work on learning what the Bible says about who you are in Christ. Just as people learning to identify counterfeit money examine real currency so they can spot the fakes, the struggler needs to fill his mind with God's Word so he can enter into his true identity as a beloved, valuable child of God.

The third step is working on the thought life, since this is where the battle is. It's important to identify Satan's lies playing as tapes in one's head, and stop the tape player! Then, deliberately replace the lies with the truth. Instead of "I'm never going to change," repeat the truthful promise that "I can do all things through Christ who strengthens me" (Phil. 4:13). Instead of obsessing over the aching and longing for the unhealthy and sinful behavior, fill your mind with praise and worship and Scripture.

Next, face the fact that it feels lousy! When we stop trying to meet our needs in our own ways, we start experiencing the emotional pain that our strongholds had covered up. When it feels really really bad, we are at that very point where God can make the biggest difference. Ask, What is my true need? What is it my heart is truly longing for? Go to Jesus and let Him meet your deepest heart-needs. Let Him direct you to get your

5

divinely-designed needs for relationship with other people met in godly ways. This is where powerful healing happens.

Ex-Ex-gays

For the last several years, people who had left homosexuality have slowly but surely gained a hearing in telling their stories. Word is getting out: change is possible!

And there are also the voices of the frustrated and disillusioned souls who tried to leave homosexuality, who tried to change, and gave up. There's even a name for it: "Ex ex-gays." Their stories are full of tremendous pain, and some have even lost their faith over it. What happened?

Well, I think the same thing that happened to people who tried AA but couldn't stop drinking, or those who tried Weigh Down Workshop but couldn't lose weight. I have a friend who was in Weigh Down Workshop, and it didn't do a thing for her. The problem is, she never made the commitment to "die to self," to use an old spiritual term.[2] She never got to the point of saying, "Jesus, I choose You over food. I choose a holy relationship with You over an unhealthy relationship with my appetite. And I will do whatever it takes to allow You to change my heart."

Many people who tried to change their homosexuality could win contests for praying and reading their Bibles. They really did try very very hard. But the prayers are often misdirected: "God, change me. Take away my desires. Let me start liking people of the opposite sex." Unfortunately, as well-intentioned as this prayer is, it's a lot like trying to get rid of dandelions in your back yard by mowing them. They keep coming back because you're not dealing with their roots. The basic cause of a homosexual orientation isn't genetics or choice; it's a wrong response to being hurt. It's about protecting oneself and trying to get legitimate needs met in ways God never intended. True change can only happen with the hard work of submitting to God, allowing Him to expose the deep hurts and needs of one's heart, which means facing horrible pain, and inviting Him to bring healing to those wounded places. That's why intimacy with Christ is the answer. A wise friend observed that homosexuality is the fruit of sinful ways of dealing with pain--sinful because they cut us off from the One who can heal and meet our needs, sinful because they place us at the center of our universe and we don't belong there. Jesus does.

I hope you can see that real change is hard and it costs a great deal because it requires strong motivation, hard work, and perseverance. But hundreds of former homosexuals have found a large degree of change, attaining abstinence from homosexual behaviors, lessening of

6

3

A Hunger
For Love

By

Dottie Ludwig

I was three-and-a-half years old when my mother died. I remember the day. I was sitting in the wood box, looking into the bedroom where I could see the bed.

The doctor and my father came out of the room together. After the doctor had gone, my father went to the table where three of my four sisters were sitting. I watched him pick up each one and comfort them. I was sitting there crying, but I was left alone, unnoticed by my dad. It doesn't do any good to feel, I decided. Nobody cares anyway. And so very early I learned to stuff my feelings.

In the following years, I lived with several different families. Part of the time I had one or two of my sisters with me; sometimes, it was just me. In these families, I perceived the mother figures to be distant and unloving. Father figures were drunk, emotionally distant, or molesting me. My only contact with my father was a monthly 30-minute visit (if that).

Often, I felt unwanted and useless. Life is unfair, I would think. Why doesn't somebody love me? I was given smaller food portions than the rest of the family, so often I was hungry. Sometimes I ate dog food; at other times, my foster father would lure me into the barn, enticing me with a candy bar. But he'd withhold it until I satisfied him sexually.

I survived those years by withdrawing into a fantasy world where I was a "superman" figure saving the world. But I never dreamed of rescuing myself. I didn't count.

During childhood, I was forced to attend church, where I heard about a God who would punish me if I did wrong. However, I also remember learning the hymn, "What A Friend We Have in Jesus" Somehow I knew there was a God who loved me.

Then, during sixth grade, I was unwillingly dragged to the church altar during a service. After that, I did everything I could to avoid church.

My first memory of hungering for love from another woman dates back to high school. We had a neighbor who would wave to me from her kitchen window and invite me into her antique shop to see her treasures. I loved to be with her, and wished that she could be my mother.

I finished high school in 1953 and entered nurse's training in Portland, Maine. Back then, homosexuality was rarely mentioned. But when I read about the subject in my psychiatric textbook, I had a fleeting thought: Maybe that's what I am.

My first involvement in lesbianism occurred after graduation when I became friends with another nurse. One night, while staying overnight at her house, she reached out to me in a sexual way. I responded positively to her advances and we began a four-year lesbian relationship. I had six relationships over the next 12 years. These women temporarily satisfied my need for love and acceptance. However, after a time, each relationship would cool down and we would drift apart.

Although I appeared normal, professional and successful on the outside, I lived with constant guilt and fear of being "found out." When a relationship would end, I'd deny that I was gay and promise myself never to enter another lesbian relationship. But sooner or later, I would respond to a physical overture from someone, which would lead to sexual and emotional enmeshment.

No one knew of my lesbian involvement, and I struggled alone with my guilt and fears. While still involved in my last relationship, however, I told my friend, "This relationship is sin, and I can no longer be involved." I believe God heard and honored that confession of my heart. I still did not know Him, but His grace was at work in me.

In 1974, I became friends with a Christian woman who told me about Jesus. Her whole Bible study group began praying for me. That fall, I became a "born-again" believer (see John 3) as God revealed Himself to me.

Finally I truly understood about sin, confessed my past immorality, and received God's forgiveness. I permanently stopped my sexual involvement with other women. However, the deep need for love--the root issue of my lesbian longings--had yet to be resolved.

As a new Christian, I had a tremendous fear of letting anyone know I had been involved in lesbianism. The gay jokes I heard among professing Christians only reinforced my fears. If they know about my past, they will reject me, I thought.

Then I became friends with another nurse who was going through a rough time. I was ecstatic when we'd do things together and looked forward to the next time we'd be together. Most of our activities were church-related, and I believe God used her to help me grow spiritually. However, I became emotionally dependent on this woman (the feelings were one-sided). There was not a physical attraction, but the emotional enmeshment was just as destructive.

God used three things to begin dealing with the roots of lesbianism in my life. First, He arranged a confrontation with my friend about my past. "How come the topic of homosexuality seems to come up so often in conversations with you and others?" she asked me. I remained silent.

"Have you ever been a homosexual?" she shouted, and I admitted the truth.

She looked at me with fire in her eyes. "And I thought I could trust you. What a hypocrite! I'm not even sure you're a Christian" She stormed out and drove off in her car as I cried to God for help.

I felt ashamed and abandoned once more. I seriously contemplated getting into my car and leaving forever. But at just the right time, my friend returned and we talked about my past. She apologized for her reaction. Later I learned that she was fearful of her own reputation since I was living with her and her children at this time. From then on, I resolved to be open about my past with any serious friendships.

Second, this friend began dating and doing other things without me. I found myself feeling jealous, hurt, possessive, and rejected. I felt abandoned and depressed. I knew of no one with whom I could share my struggles.

One day I was praying when the Lord brought to mind the words, "inordinate affection" (see Col. 3:5). I sensed that God was talking about the underlying dynamic of my relationship with my roommate, and that I needed to repent of it. Before this, I had only associated lesbianism with sexual involvement. Now I began to understand how my need for healthy same-sex love had become distorted. I asked the Lord to forgive me and help me have His love for my friend.

"Often, I felt unwanted and useless. Life is unfair, I would think. Why doesn't somebody love me?"

Another night I told the Lord, "I don't care if I never have another friend in my life. You alone are enough!" I meant those words, and experienced a release from the emotional bondage I'd felt in my heart.

Third, God prevented me from helping others so He could show me my worth and value in Him. He showed me that I needed to learn how to receive. At the time I was physically helpless, emotionally drained, and very needy. It humbled me to learn that God and His people accepted me, even when I had nothing to give.

I knew that I had to start forming some other relationships and felt God urging me to attend a women's Bible study at church. I went many times in sheer obedience, not hearing much of what was said, but simply receiving all the Lord was doing in me through His Word and His people. Gradually I began going for coffee afterward with some of the women. God used those times to show me I could have friends without all the emotional baggage that I'd had in the past. And He began filling my same-sex love deficit through several women--not just one. I even shared my lesbian past with the group, and was still accepted. Inner healing prayer and healing of memories were also a part of my recovery. I forgave those who had traumatized me in childhood, but the Lord alone did the healing; unfortunately, all the people had died, leaving no opportunity for restoration of any relationships.

I walked away from lesbianism 27 years ago, and God dealt with its roots over a seven-year period after I became a Christian. Since the early 1980s, I have noticed some major changes in my attitude toward men. I no longer fear them, and find myself attracted to them.

Instead of searching for love, I have learned to receive love from my Heavenly Father. In being able to receive, I have embraced an essential part of my femininity. God has filled my hunger for love--and I remain amazed at all He has done.

"A Hunger for Love" by Dottie Ludwig, Copyright © 1994, All rights reserved. Used with permission.

(AP Photo/Abby Brack, Copyright 2004 used with permission)
Massachusetts Gov. Mitt Romney tells reporters Monday, March 29, 2004 that he
will ask the state's Supreme Judicial Court--which had ruled that gay couples had
a constitutional right to marry --to delay its decision until after the constitutional
amendment process has run its course.

4

A New Life

By

Linda D. Carter

I grew up as the youngest in a family of six children. For as long as I can remember, I found myself attracted to women. As I grew older, these feelings became stronger and stronger. I didn't know how to explain what I was feeling inside. I was raised in a strong and loving Christian home. I knew that because sexual and other "worldly" matters were never to be discussed, I could never talk about what was going on inside of me; so I carried this secret for years.

When I was in high school, all my friends had boyfriends except me. I never felt comfortable dressing up and wearing make-up, as my girlfriends did (except on Sundays). I was much more comfortable in blue jeans and t-shirts. When I got to the eleventh grade, I had my first boyfriend. I really liked this guy, but I still had feelings of attraction to other girls. I tried to fight these feelings. I wanted so badly to be "normal" like all my friends were.

In the fall of 1980, I enrolled in a junior college. It was at this time that I had my first sexual encounter with a woman. She seemed to be everything I wanted in a man, but I found it instead in a woman. But gradually she started having affairs with other women, and they introduced her to their friends. She wanted to try it all: other women, drugs and alcohol. I wanted a committed relationship with her alone, but that was not enough for her. What had started out being so wonderful soon became what seemed to be her betrayal of me. I realized that she'd had a lot of experience in this lifestyle, whereas she was my first girlfriend. Our relationship ended up in chaos and confusion. I tried everything to win her back, but nothing worked. In the end, she was involved with multiple sexual partners. I never wanted any of that kind of life, so we went our separate ways. I was completely devastated in the end.

The pain I felt after our breakup began to show itself in my obsessive drinking and partying. I did not want another lover, so I started going to gay bars and house parties. I met a lot of other women, but was afraid to get seriously involved with any of them at first. Eventually, I did begin dating again and become involved with six other women. None of these relationships lasted more than one year. I was living the "gay life," but instead of feeling good about it -- I felt trapped.

During those years, I felt as if I were riding on a roller coaster. I prayed and I prayed to God, "When is this ride going to end? Are you ever going to change me?" It seemed as if God was not hearing my prayers, no matter how hard I prayed. Finally, I just stopped altogether. I did not know this at the time, but my mother never stopped her prayers for me. She "stood in the gap" for me. Even though we had never discussed my lesbianism, she knew. She was a real woman of God and a true and loving mother, one who knew her children well.

In the spring of 1995, my mother passed away and went to be with the Lord. Shortly afterward, my life seemed to change. My mother's death had left a huge void in my life. I realized that something really important was missing. I did not know what was happening to me at the time, but I know now that I entered a time of great depression.

The following winter, I felt that God was really beginning to help me come to terms with my desire for women. Slowly, it began to decrease. My lesbian friends would call me and ask me to go out with them, but I began turning down their invitations. That was a real change, going from a woman who had always gone to gay parties and clubs, to one whose interest in these activities was disappearing! The next step was that I stopped even taking calls from my old friends and eventually changed my phone number to an unlisted one.

"During those years, I felt as if I were riding on a roller coaster. I prayed and I prayed to God, 'When is this ride going to end?'"

One day, I telephoned these friends and actually told them that I could no longer hang out with them, and I told them why. What had taken place was that I surrendered my life to God. I shared this with them, and they wanted to know what I was going to do with my life. I shared Jesus Christ with them and asked them if they wanted to accept Christ as I had done. They all said no to me and told me the same thing, though in different ways. What they expressed to me was that they were not ready to do that. I told them that I loved them with the love of Jesus, and I assured them that I would be praying for them.

I began to seek the Lord in every way I knew how: through Christian television, prayer, and in reading the Bible. I noticed that my desires for women began to fade away, and soon I was not struggling with them at all. I believe this happened because I was truly focused on the Lord. I was hungry for Him.

I started dating men, and met one man whose company I especially enjoyed. He seemed different from any man I had ever met. I enjoyed his sense of humor, his kindness to me, and our conversations. He was a man who was greatly respected. Being in his company, I never felt a drawing to be with my former friends. I had a feeling somewhere inside of me that this could end up in our being married.

What actually happened was that we had a "long-distance" relationship. By that time, I was away going to college. We both traveled back and forth to see each other. We spoke often by telephone. I felt even more strongly that he was the man for me! Then we became sexually involved, and I got pregnant. Instead of marriage, he broke our relationship. All my hopes were destroyed, and I was alone again. I really thought that this man would be the one to change my life, but that did not happen. After the birth of my son, I was very disillusioned and maybe as a result of that, I ended up going back into the lesbian life. But, thanks be to God, it was only for a time! The Lord pursued me and brought me out again.

My son has been a great blessing in my life, and I thank God for him. If you ask me if I miss living as a lesbian, my answer to you would be, "No way!" God created me a woman and has healed me of a terrible curse that tried to tell me otherwise. I praise Him every day for it, and I know He has forgiven me for trying to go back to the old ways for a time.

I had wondered when, how or if I would ever share my past with my son. In December of 1998, God provided me that opportunity. We had gone to visit my sister-in-law and her husband in Alabama. We stayed there overnight, and during that visit, I knew the time was right for him to know. I was very fearful of his reaction at first. I thought he might resent me or judge me. After I finished sharing, I asked him if he needed to ask me anything. He said that I had answered everything for him. Instead of resenting me, he told me that no matter what, he loved me. He also told me that he was not ashamed of me. I was glad that I had been the one to tell him these things, rather than his hearing it from someone else. When we returned home from our visit, I was asked to share my testimony at our church. While driving home from church with my son the night I told my story, he said, "Mom, I am so proud of you!" I felt a huge load had been lifted from me that night.

God gave me another opportunity to share my past -- this time with my two closest friends. When I told them, both of them assured me of their love for me, no matter what I had done in the past. They let me know that our friendship would always be there. When they shared that there was nothing that could change how much they loved me, I felt wonderful, and somehow very special.

I now have such peace and joy in my heart. God is working in my life with all His power. God created me to be a woman, and deep inside of me, He has assured me that this is what I am. Perhaps God has allowed me to go through all the things I did so that I could help others who struggle with homosexual temptations -- to let them know that he loves every one of them, but that He hates all sin. People need to know and to see and hear how God can save and deliver. What He has done in my life, I believe He can do in your life, no matter what problems you have.

"I noticed that my desires for women began to fade away, and soon I was not struggling with them at all."

The Enemy, Satan, is a liar. He comes "to steal, kill and destroy." God comes to give us life, joy and peace. He wants us to experience freedom. Jesus is the way out of all our struggles with sin. Satan is already defeated. I encourage you to read Leviticus 20:13, and Romans 1:24-28. These scriptures give insight as to what God has to say about homosexuals. Homosexuality does not come from God. Remember also Philippians 4:13, "I can do all things through Christ, who strengthens me."

Friends, be encouraged! You can make it. To God be the glory for redeeming my life from destruction!

"A New Life" by Linda D. Carter, www.Exodus-International.org. Copyright © 2003, Exodus International. All rights reserved. Used with permission.

(AP Photo/Lisa Poole, Copyright 2004, used with permission)

Rev. Joshua Cotter, of the Unification Church in Bridgeport, Conn., center, and George Welles, of the Church of Our Savior, in Milton, Mass., right, protest against same-sex marriage and civil unions, Monday, March 29, 2004, at the Massachusetts Statehouse in Boston.

5

A Dream Come True

By

Alan Chambers

I dreamed about everything good. I dreamed of being loved, accepted, and secure. I dreamed about commitment and relationship. But, I knew lonely. I knew what it was like not to fit in and to be teased to tears. I knew what it was like to watch the boys on the playground and feel such anxiety and insecurity about joining them that I literally would do anything to avoid it. I knew what it was like to play with the girls with whom I outwardly had more in common. I knew what it was like to be different from the other boys my age and to have an insatiable need to be accepted and liked by them. I knew the pain of molestation. I knew what it was like to believe the lie that molestation was my fault because I let it happen. I knew what it was like to feel shame and pain because a part of me wanted it to happen again because if nothing else, he had chosen me! I knew what it was like to feel important and desirable to an older guy, even if it was only for a moment behind a locked door, under the guise of secrecy, confusion and stolen innocence. I knew what it was like to be so emotionally hungry for male love, affirmation and attention that the dirtiest of acts satisfied a portion of my hunger. I knew what it felt like to believe that my longing for male love and acceptance wore the name "sex." I knew what it was like to come to the realization that I was a homosexual even though I had never asked for my same sex attractions. I knew what it was like to be called "homo," "fag," and "queer" until I believed it was the truth. I dreamed of more, but lived on less.

I heard that Jesus loved me and gave His life for me and I came to know Him as my personal savior at the age of 6. I was ready to be loved by Him and to belong to His family. By the time I was 10 or 11 I began to hear at church that "homosexuals could not share in God's Kingdom" but under no circumstances did I hear that "such were some of you" (I Corinthians 6:9-11) which was 2000 year old evidence that homosexuals could change. I believed that there was no hope for me. I was a "homosexual" first, last and always. The church wanted nothing to do with me, I thought, so why would Jesus. Thus began a long process of trying to do all I could to gain His and everyone else's approval. I attended church every time the doors were open. I was a leader in my youth group. I studied my Bible. I went on mission trips. Nothing I did made those feelings go away. I prayed night after night for years that God would take away my homosexuality only to wake up morning after morning with those same longings. In fact, they were growing stronger. I was told that if I "nailed my sin to the cross" or "laid it at the altar" or simply "obeyed" or "read my Bible more" Jesus would take my burden away. Nothing was working. Disillusioned, I was desperate. I remember going into my parent's room nightly to see if they had been raptured, taken to heaven, without me. As a teenage driver, I would close my eyes as I went through blinking railroad crossings hoping a train would hit me. I was so angry with God for giving me a need for something that He condemned. I was living with a secret, utterly unacceptable and believing I was bound for Hell because my feelings were not changing.

This was my daily reality until 1990 when I attended a youth conference and the speaker said, "There is a young man sitting in the audience who thinks he is gay. He's been molested. He thinks the only way out is suicide. If that is you, I want to talk to you." When I went forward, he told me what I had never heard before in conjunction with the knowledge of my homosexual feelings, "God loves you--no matter what." Though it conflicted with what I had been taught and I could not understand how, I knew he was right. God loved me. The speaker also re-introduced me to I Corinthians 6:9-11 and gave me hope for change. I was referred to a nearby counseling center where I heard about Eleutheros (now Exchange Ministries), the local Exodus member ministry.

"I believed that there was no hope for me. I was a "homosexual" first, last and always."

I began counseling and attending support groups in late 1990 at the age of 18. I desired to make it work. The purpose of counseling and support groups is to first help you look at yourself and understand why you do the things you do and then to help you make better choices. It brings up old memories and wounds and makes you vulnerable. Six months into it, I was a wreck; I still could not get past the idea that "Mr. Right" might be out there ready to love and accept me. Before I was able to make wiser choices and after a very difficult counseling session one afternoon, I met someone who invited me to hang out with him and his friends. It sounded good to relax and have a good time. We went to a gay bar. For the first time, I found acceptance there for what was to me my greatest source of shame. I savored the openness. I did not have to hide the fact that I was gay. I had found, in part anyway, what I had only dreamed about. If not love, security and commitment at least I had acceptance. I began a weekly regime that entailed three nights a week at Eleutheros, three nights a week at the gay bar, and one day of rest.

During this time, I stumbled across a place where anonymous sexual encounters occurred. The sex didn't involve a relationship, but at least I was desirable to someone for ten minutes. Sex was a counterfeit to the love and security I desired. I became addicted. Later I would learn the scripture, "to the hungry, even what is bitter tastes sweet" (Proverbs 27:7). In spite of the sex, I continued to crave relationship more. I was lonelier and angrier than ever. No matter how hard I tried to reconcile my newfound lifestyle with my Christian faith, I believed that homosexuality was wrong. I was in perpetual conflict.

Easter Sunday 1991 found me alone in a gay bar waiting for my gay friends who would never come. As clearly as He ever has, God began to speak to me. He began by reminding me of what the speaker at the conference had told me: He loved me--no matter what. He told me that if I chose to live a gay life forever He would still love me. I was His child. You may be thinking there has to be a "but" coming. You are right. The Lord said, "The life you have found might be good, but good is the enemy of My best." The Lord climbed down into the hole I had dug for myself and promised me His best. I told Him that I believed Him and that I wanted nothing more than to please Him, but I was tired. I could not fight alone anymore. I needed help. At that moment, two friends from church walked through the doors of the bar. They paid the cover charge and told me that God had prompted them to come and help me. We walked out together. My friend Andy Comiskey has said, "We don't need judges standing over us. We need brothers and sisters walking beside us." That Easter Sunday night in 1991 the Lord personally sent a brother and sister in the flesh to walk beside me on my journey out of homosexuality.

It took me years to realize that what I dreamed of was within me all along. I found my security in a God who accepted me as I was, loved me enough to talk to me in my dirtiest condition yet not leave me there, and showed His commitment to me by providing the help I needed to get out in a tangible way. He was a God I could trust and follow.

I chose to obey Him over my feelings. I began trusting Him instead of holding onto ungodly ways of meeting my needs. I learned what He said about my homosexual struggle. It was okay to hurt and to desire, that the need for love and acceptance from a man was not bad, but rather an illegitimate way to meet a legitimate need. He taught me that sex was not created to meet my needs--only He, my heavenly Father, could do that. He let me know that all the times I cried out to Him, He had been there with an answer. I learned the necessity of forgiveness: to accept the forgiveness that God offered me and to offer forgiveness to those who had hurt me.

I recommitted myself to the process I had begun a year and a half earlier, attending support groups and seeing a counselor. I discovered some of the underlying issues that contributed to my same sex attractions. I found a church that truly represented His heart with people in it who were willing not only to tell me the truth that homosexuality was a sin, but who lived out God's kindness and tolerance that led to my true repentance (Romans 2:4). I began to share my experiences with those whom I loved the most: my brother and his wife, my parents, friends, church members, and eventually the rest of my family. I found that after telling them my deepest darkest secret, when they knew that part of me and still told me that they loved me, it was if I had never heard those words before. It was acceptance, security, love, and commitment on the deepest level.

Gradually, my will and then my desires changed. I no longer needed gay sex. I had pure relationships with men and women that far exceeded any encounter I had ever had. My hurt was real and a struggle free life is not what I have found. I have found freedom in the hope that after this short life, God will fulfill His promise of healing to completion. I can also expect to find, "the goodness of the Lord in the land of the living" (Psalm 27:13), as well. It is not just in heaven that we will experience His goodness; it is here in this lifetime.

"The Lord climbed down into the hole I had dug for myself and promised me His best."

In 1998 the ultimate earthly dream came true when I married my best friend. Leslie is the embodiment of all I consider to be godly, pure and beautiful. She is not my diploma for healing, nor is she proof that I have changed. She is, however, evidence of God's grace in my life, a part of the 'best' that God promised me back in that gay bar. God uses her in my life to bring constant encouragement as I grow in my manhood. I am a better man today because of my life with her and because of God's continuing work in me. My life with Leslie is abundantly more than I could have ever hoped for and the dearest earthly blessing God could have ever given me aside from His Son.

Today I am experiencing what I used to only dream about but never found in the gay life. I have a loving wife, a wonderful relationship with my family, godly friendships, a church who stands for the truth and understands God's grace, and a ministry where I can serve Him who made all of my dreams come true. It humbles me to think that my story may be just the sign that someone needs to get up and walk out of whatever trap in which they find themselves. God knew my deepest needs, and He is meeting them as I follow Him. He can do the same for you. We cannot help but be changed as we make Him Lord of our life and experience His love for us. He has done great things!

"A Dream Come True" by Alan Chambers, www.Exodus-International.org . Copyright © 2003, Exodus International. All rights reserved. Used with permission.

(AP Photo/Steven Senne, Copyright 2004, used with permission)

Rev. Anne Rousseau, of the United Church of Christ, left, Sonia Chang, of Boston, center, and Rev. Patricia Walton, also of the UCC, right, speak in favor of same-sex marriage outside the House Chamber at the Statehouse in Boston, Monday, March 29, 2004, as legislators debate a constitutional ban on same-sex marriage inside the chamber.

6

Delivered From Despair

By

Tom Cole

I was the third son in a family of six children. My parents had been hoping for a girl; from the time I was very young, my mother told me that, if I had been a girl, my name would have been Debbie.

My lack of interest in contact sports alienated me from the other boys in the neighborhood. When we lined up to pick teams, I would be last and someone would remark, "Oh no, we got stuck with Cole. He's a sissy." Each time my heart grew colder and harder.

Ugly Names

As far back as I can remember, I was called names like fag, queer and sissy. My gentle demeanor and compassionate nature, on the other hand, made me compatible with the neighborhood girls; soon they became my sole source of friendship.

One day in fifth grade, our teacher tried an experiment in communication. She had the class gather in a circle and talk about the things that bothered them. Suddenly I became the subject of conversation. The boys in the class began to complain, "Cole is a fag. We don't want to sit by him or work on projects with him." When the teacher asked me how I felt about these comments, I ran from the classroom, crying and feeling sick to my stomach. School became a dichotomy: I loved to learn, but I feared the daily harassment.

One day I came home scraped and beaten, and my father said, "If you're going to make it in this world, you're going to have to fight."

"But Daddy, I'm afraid to fight." In response, his face turned red with anger. He forced my hands up and started jousting with his fists, but I only stood there and cried. I hated my father for forcing me to be something I could never be. I despised other males and vowed in my heart that I would never be like them.

"A New Game"

Then an older boy in the neighborhood began to show attention to me and I was elated. But one day when we were playing in his back yard, he led me into his tent and said, "I have a new game for us to play." He began to undress and told me to do the same. As he sexually molested me, I felt fear, revulsion and the need to get away. Mixed with these negative feelings were sensations of physical pleasure. Afterward I avoided my friend and buried the incident deep in my memory.

About age 12, I began to experiment sexually with other boys in the neighborhood. One neighbor and I began a six-year physical relationship.

I felt cheapened by these experiences; now I had friends, but I saw that they only wanted me for their sexual release.

Visiting Gay Bars

In college, I majored in music and drama. I joined a vocal jazz ensemble and met a male singer who was "out of the closet" with his homosexuality. One day I asked if he would take me to a gay bar, and he readily agreed. I felt fear and excitement as I anticipated the experience. I was 19 years old, but most people thought I looked 14 or 15.

When we entered the bar, I noticed that many of the men were staring at me. I felt like an animal on display in the zoo. But I also loved the attention. I met a much older man and we planned a date for the following week. He lavished attention on me, and I loved it. But after a few times together, he seemed to lose interest in me; the next week, I saw him with another guy who looked even younger than me.

"As far back as I can remember, I was called names like fag, queer and sissy."

I found it difficult to enter into a long-term relationship with other men. One time I asked a group of gay friends, "Don't you think it's a little strange that all we talk about and think about is sex? Is that what the average heterosexual is like?" No one responded, but I knew that what we were experiencing wasn't right.

A Shocking Discovery

One night I was shocked to see my younger brother at the club. We had both experienced many of the same things in our lives and we shared a close friendship until his death eight years later in a tragic car accident.

I saw my brother in a seemingly healthy gay relationship and thought, Maybe it can work after all. But then I watched the relationship deteriorate to a violent end, and I lost hope for a long-term gay relationship. From the age of 19 until I was 26, I had 300-400 sexual partners. Depression set in; I began to drink and use cocaine to deaden the loneliness.

One night, in total despair, I decided to end my life. I took a large amount of painkillers and a fifth of vodka. I awoke the next day feeling like I had been run over by a truck. I was alive -- but still miserable.

Relationship with Jesus

Soon after, I met a woman at work named Rosie who constantly talked about a personal relationship with Jesus. When I brought up some of my New Age beliefs, she always responded in love--and never condemned me as a homosexual. One night she said, "My husband and I will be praying for you."

I was shocked. "You pray for me?" I asked.

"Yes," she said. "We pray for you every night."

As she was leaving, she added, "Tom, I love you." Something broke inside; the love of God reached out through Rosie and touched my heart. I hid my head under a counter, pretending to clean, while I wept.

Finding Something Different in Church

Within a few weeks, I asked Rosie if I could attend church with her. That Sunday, I sensed something different. People hugged one another and sang with such love to Jesus. At the end of the service, I went forward to receive Jesus Christ into my life.

I began telling people of my life before Christ and asking for their prayers. Then I met Donna, a former lesbian, at a prayer meeting and we began a prayer partnership. After two years of studying the Bible and praying together, I knew my feelings for her were more than friendship.

One day Donna came to visit me at work. For the first time, I noticed her well-endowed figure and felt strongly attracted to her. I realized that, at age 26, I was experiencing something most boys go through at puberty. Soon Donna and I were dating. Three months later, we were married.

Entering Marriage--and Finding New Problems

Our first year of marriage was torture as my insecurities poured out. I began to seek solace in phone sex with men. Then I heard a broadcast on homosexuality, featuring an interview with Dr. Elizabeth Moberly. As she spoke about same-gender deficits, I realized that I had many close female friends in my life, but no significant male friendships. I asked God to send men to me with whom I could share my struggles. The Lord was faithful and sent two men within the next year. They were gentle and compassionate, and held me accountable.

God also sent me another friend to whom I would have been strongly attracted back in my gay life. I was nervous and uneasy as we attended a weekend conference together. I decided to share my insecurities with him and said I was afraid of getting close to other men.

He responded with wisdom and gentle love. "Just because I've never struggled with homosexuality doesn't mean that I don't fear intimacy." Then he explained that men often talk about weather or sports to avoid discussing their feelings and what is really happening in their lives. I was shocked and relieved. Slowly I was learning that I could be intimate with a man without being sexual with him.

One night, in total despair, I decided to end my life. I took a large amount of painkillers and a fifth of vodka. I awoke the next day feeling like I had been run over by a truck. I was alive -- but still miserable.

When my wife gave birth to our first child, I asked God, "How do I raise a son?" I sensed His response in my heart: "Just love him." Today Isaac is 100 percent all boy. Shortly after him came another son, then two daughters. My children are one of life's greatest joys.

Joy in Helping Others

As my wife and I both found freedom from a gay past, we began to minister to others seeking the same experience. Four years ago, we joined the board of directors of Reconciliation, our local Exodus ministry in Detroit. Two years later, I became the director.

Today our vision is to help Christians who long for change in their homosexual desires. We don't force our beliefs on anyone, but seek to display the compassion of Jesus Christ to anyone who is interested. I know His love can draw others out of despair, just as He did for me.

"Delivered from Despair" by Tom Cole, www.Exodus-International.org . Copyright © 2003, Exodus International. All rights reserved. Used with permission.

35

(AP Photo/Lisa Poole, Copyright 2004, used with permission)

Keith OByrne, of Boston, right, makes his pro gay marriage case to Mikael Duval, of Plymouth, Mass., left, who is against gay marriage, outside the Statehouse as the constitutional convention continued to debate the gay marriage issue, Monday, March 29, 2004, in Boston.

7

God Healed My Marriage

By

Alan Medinger

During a recent quiet time, the Lord showed me what my life might have been like today. I envisioned myself living alone downtown--lonely and desperate, still going after that which could not satisfy, seeking from other men that which they did not have to give.

Willa, my wife, was living somewhere else, the anger and hurt in her life still hidden beneath the surface. I saw our younger daughter, Beth, daily expressing an anger towards a father who had never understood her needs and who had finally abandoned her. Our older daughter, Laura, carried a deep sadness for a father she loved very much. Our son, Steven, had not been born at all.

A New Man

But that is not the way my life is. On the night of November 26, 1974, a new man was born. Perhaps it would be more accurate to say that a boy was reborn and started to grow into a man.

In my background were most of the ingredients typically seen as contributing to homosexuality: an unplanned child, parents who were hoping for a girl, an older brother who met the father's ideal more than I, and a father with severe emotional problems which caused him to barely be able to cope with life himself, much less meet the needs of his son. Now I know that these factors did not cause my homosexuality. Rather, my responses to these factors influenced me in that direction.

Lifelong Attractions to Men

My attraction to men goes back almost as far as I can remember. I suppose I was about twelve years old when I started acting out my homosexual attractions. But, growing up in the 1940's and 50's, there was not a visible gay subculture, a homosexual lifestyle, to which I could aspire. I always assumed I would marry and do the best I could. My wife Willa and I had grown up neighbors, dated through high school, and then in college became more serious.

She was a wonderful, popular girl and I believed we could have a good life together. We were married and things went well in the early years. But about the fifth year of marriage, after our two daughters were born and the normal family and career pressures started to build, I again became homosexually active. I was involved for the next ten years.

During those years I believed that, except for this one great, dark area in my life, I had it all together. I was successful in business, a pillar of the church, and had a wonderful family, including foster children we took in.

Theologically, I had it pretty well figured out. All men and women commit sin, and this was my particular area of weakness.

Hating My Homosexuality

This may be hard for many to understand, but I hated my homosexuality more than anyone could imagine. But even worse was the thought of giving it up. I don't know why. Was I really seeking love from another man? To be worth something to a man? To possess another's manhood? Perhaps it was all of these, but sex with another man met some need, provided some relief or escape that I felt I had to have.

> # "My attraction to men goes back almost as far as I can remember. I suppose I was about twelve years old when I started acting out my homosexual attractions."

I figured that if I just kept it moderately under control, God's scorecard on me would tally up in my favor and I would be okay. But everything was not under control. The compulsion was increasing and my going out became more frequent and reckless. My marriage was coming apart at the seams. I finally was no longer able to function heterosexually. Willa figured out what the problem was, but decided not to confront me.

The Power of Prayer

My wife, of course, was desperately unhappy during those years. She joined a prayer group of mature Christian women who were true prayer warriors. Although she did not tell them the specific nature of the problem, they started praying for our marriage. Willa began sensing that she should let go of me. If the marriage were to fall apart, and me with it, she was to let it happen. She was able to let go of me, spiritually and emotionally.

Not long after this, a friend asked me to attend a prayer meeting. I resisted for a long time, but finally agreed to go. He told me, "What the Lord has for you is far better than anything you could imagine." When I heard that, a great peace came over me.

39

A Great Change

To a casual onlooker, nothing spectacular happened that November night. But inside of me, a great change occurred. As the large group of two or three hundred people were praying and praising God aloud, I quietly surrendered my life, including my homosexuality, to Jesus Christ. I admitted my helplessness, that my life was a wreck, that I was willing to let Him do whatever He would with my life.

Beginning the following day, I started to recognize that a whole bundle of miracles had occurred. Gone were the homosexual fantasies which seemed to have seldom left my waking mind over the previous 25 years. I felt a love for Willa that I never knew was possible.

Perhaps most important of all, God was no longer a faraway scorekeeper. He was a Savior who had come down from His heaven and brought me salvation. Jesus loved me and I loved Him so very much. I know for the first time what it was to love and be loved in return.

At the time, I felt that what God had done was a total healing, and it is true that the sexual pull towards other men was gone. But homosexuality is more than having sex with someone of the same gender. Closer to the root is a deep brokenness, almost a stillbirth in our manhood or womanhood. Somehow as a small boy, I had closed a door to my growth into manhood. God helped me open it again.

Growth Into Manhood

My conversion marked the resumption of my growth into manhood. God has worked wonderfully to remove my great sense of inadequacy around "straight" men, those who have never experienced homosexuality. He has enabled me to become an initiator and a leader, roles which I dreaded at one time. In a beautifully gentle way, God has been shifting the roles my wife and I take, so that I can assume my proper headship in our family.

Because of the sudden nature of my healing from homosexuality, I am often asked, "How complete is your healing...really?" In reply, I can say it has stood the test of time and has borne the fruit of a blessed marriage.

I have not been homosexually tempted during the past ten years. By temptation, I mean seriously desiring or considering a sexual act with another of the same sex. I did carry beyond my initial healing some desire for an older, stronger man to "take care of me." That too is now gone, and I see men as brothers, not as father-protectors.

Naturally, I have avoided literature, movies and other situations which could arouse homosexual lust. When they are encountered, as they will be, or when someone I am counseling describes the circumstances of a sexual fall, it does sometimes give rise to some sexual feelings. However, those are minor and are diminishing with the passing of time. I may still take a look at a good-looking man, but God has shown me in the past few years that this is based on envy and habits from the past. As I repent of the envy and continue to thank God for the way He made me, this too is becoming less frequent.

I am frequently asked the question that unfortunately is often considered the acid test: "Are you sexually aroused by women in general?" No, I am not. I love my wife, and we have had a wonderful and enjoyable sexual/ romantic relationship since my healing. But she is the only woman with whom I wish to have sex. Sexual intercourse is meant to be an expression of love between two people in the context of a lifetime commitment. It is only because of the Fall that men have problems lusting for women outside of that committed relationship. Therefore, it seems unlikely that God would replace my homosexuality with a fallen heterosexuality. I thank Him that He has spared me that battle.

"To a casual onlooker, nothing spectacular happened that November night. But inside of me, a great change occurred"

I'm so thankful that the picture of "what might have been" in my life today has not occurred. I am involved full time in ministry to homosexuals. Willa and I are working together in this ministry. We are looking forward to celebrating our twenty-fifth wedding anniversary. Our two daughters are now in college and Stephen, our son who "would not have been," is eight years old and doing well. And his father loves him very much.

"God Healed my Marriage" by Alan Medinger, www.Exodus-International.org . Copyright © 2003, Exodus International. All rights reserved. Used with permission.

(AP Photo/Lisa Poole, Copyright 2004, used with permission)

Protesters support gay marriage during a rally outside the Massachusetts Statehouse, Wednesday, Feb. 11, 2004, in Boston, as the state legislature convenes a constitutional convention to debate a proposal to rewrite the state constitution to ban same-sex marriages.

8

My Experience With AIDS

By

Robert Winter

Have a seat, Bob," my doctor said. He paused, looking at me soberly. "Your test result came back positive. You have been exposed to the virus that causes AIDS.

"Now, it's important for you to realize what this means," he continued. "It doesn't mean you will necessarily get AIDS. But the HIV virus is in your blood. As a result, your immune system has created antibodies to it."

The year was 1985. It had been two years since I decided to leave the gay lifestyle, but now my secret fear was coming true. The AIDS virus had invaded my body.

First Homosexual Experience

I was in the eighth grade when I had my first homosexual experience with one of the older guys at boarding school. My confused adolescent fantasies included sex with men and women after that. A second homosexual encounter during my first year of Bible college seemed to confirm what I'd suspected for years. *I must be gay, I thought.*

My friends seldom talked about sex. I felt they could never help or tolerate someone with my feelings. Homosexuality seemed too evil a subject to talk about. So I hid my problem, saying nothing to anyone.

Finally, I couldn't stand the hypocrisy I felt between my outward Christianity and my inner homosexual longings. The gay lifestyle appeared to offer love and acceptance, a place where I would finally belong. I quit college and plunged into the gay life. Over the next 12 years, I got heavily involved in drugs, alcohol and deep levels of sexual perversion in an attempt to deny the emptiness in my life. Satan twisted my soul and personality until my behavior disgusted and shocked even me. But instead of love, acceptance and belonging, I only developed deeper levels of insecurity and self-hatred.

By the age of 30 I had the things that should have made me happy: a good job, my own home, and a 21-year-old lover who really cared for me. Yet none of this satisfied me. I wasn't even capable of being faithful to my lover and ended the relationship. All the things society implied would make me happy had failed.

A New Hope

One day, my mother gave me a sermon tape from her church. For the first time, I heard of men and women who had come out of homosexuality. God used that tape to soften my heart and to give me hope that change was possible. I went for counseling and experienced the power of God as He began changing and restoring my life.

For several months, my homosexual feelings vanished. My gay struggles are over, I thought naively. I'll never be troubled by homosexuality again. But then all the old feelings came back. I sought counseling at church, but the counselor didn't really understand homosexuality. He felt that I shouldn't share with my friends what I was going through, and this made things even worse.

Inner Conflict

Soon I started going to parks and places where I could engage in anonymous sexual behavior. The conflict inside was terrible. Even though I wanted to serve the Lord, I couldn't stop my sin. The pain I felt was like slashing myself with a knife. I knew God held me responsible for my actions, but I felt powerless to break the addiction.

"The year was 1985. It had been two years since I decided to leave the gay lifestyle, but now my secret fear was coming true. The AIDS virus had invaded my body."

Because of the strain on my life and emotions, I started to seriously consider suicide. Thankfully God put people into my life to encourage me. Although they didn't know much about homosexuality, they gave me unconditional love and helped me to persevere. I cried out to God, and couldn't understand why He didn't seem to answer. Only later did I realize He was preparing help for me all along.

God brought me to a ministry for people who struggle with homosexuality. Their 18-week course changed my life by restoring my hope. For the first time I met people who had successfully left the gay lifestyle, including some who were happily married. The possibility of change and wholeness became a reality to me.

Testing Positive

But during this period of new hope, my energy level plummeted. I went for tests. Two weeks later, my doctor informed me I tested positive to the HIV virus. It didn't seem fair and I cried out to God. "I'm finally getting some help and now this!" Initially I felt angry at God and considered going back into the lifestyle. I had tried so hard, and now I might get AIDS. In my anger I even had thoughts of just going crazy and having sex with as many people as possible, as some sort of twisted revenge on God and life. It seemed that God had deserted me.

"If God genuinely loved me, He wouldn't have let me get sick," I said to myself. I felt He was punishing me for not being good enough. As I worked through these feelings, I realized it was my choice to go into the gay lifestyle. My illness was a result of my sexual sin.

Also I realized my exposure to the virus had probably occurred before I returned to the Lord. He knew I would become ill and brought me help because He loved me. Jesus died on the cross for me and forgave my sins, but He didn't promise to take away all the physical consequences of those sins. When I tested positive in 1985, I was told that only about 20% of the people who tested positive would actually get AIDS. Currently the figure quoted is around 70% and some physicians believe it will eventually be 100%. From a purely medical viewpoint the outlook is not encouraging.

Fortunately there is a great deal of work being done to find a cure. The doctors are getting better at prolonging and improving the life of AIDS patients. Even more important is the fact that God is not limited by man's knowledge.

As a Christian I know all things are possible with Christ. I believe that God does physically heal people today. I have learned to be persistent in praying for my physical healing and to believe that it is possible. After all, if God has the power to create this entire universe and to raise people from the dead, He can certainly destroy a small virus in my body.

Yet I have also learned not to equate being healed with receiving God's love. I know deep in my heart that God loves me. He will do what's best for my life.

In June of 1987, I developed PCP (Pneumocystis Carinii Pneumonia) which classified me as having "full-blown" AIDS. I don't know if God is going to heal me or take me home, but He is always there to comfort me.

What I've Learned

One of the lessons God taught me was not to suppress the emotions of fear and grief. At first I tried, but that only made things worse. Instead I try to follow the example of David in the Psalms. He is always honest with God about where he is at. First he is honest about how he feels and then he focuses on how wonderful God is and what He has done.

It has been better for me to cry with my loved ones about how much it will hurt if God takes me home, rather then glossing over it and never discussing it. Only when I am willing to face fear and grief can Jesus come into the situation and bring me comfort. But if I refuse to talk about my feelings, communication and intimacy with my loved ones are blocked.

Eternal Perspective

My life on earth will seem like a moment when compared with eternity. Learning to deal with AIDS and to trust the Lord since my diagnosis has brought me deeper peace and joy than I thought possible.

"Yet I have also learned not to equate being healed with receiving God's love. I know deep in my heart that God loves me. He will do what's best for my life."

Through facing trials, fears and pain, I have learned that God is always there to comfort me and help me through the hard times. If I let myself remain in an attitude of self-pity or anger, it blocks the peace, joy and comfort that He has for me.

Regardless of whether I am healed or taken to heaven, I know that facing AIDS has brought me closer to God than ever. The more I can develop a meaningful relationship with Him in this life, the better I will be able to serve Him during eternity.

"My Experience with AIDS" by Robert Winter, www.Exodus-International.org . Copyright © 2003, Exodus International. All rights reserved. Used with permission.

AP Photo/Julia Malakie, Copyright 2004, used with permission)

Hundreds of people attend a rally against the possible amendment to the Massachusetts constitution to ban same-sex marriage, at the Statehouse in Boston, Tuesday, Feb. 10, 2004. People from around the globe converged on the Statehouse while legislators worked to find some middle ground on the issue

9
Who Am I?

By

Bob Ragan

I did not become acquainted with the word "homosexual" until I was in high school. I knew, however, that it described the feelings I had experienced throughout my childhood.

Same-sex attractions and feelings had been around since I could remember. I assumed that this is how I was born and these feelings defined who I was as a person. I heard no discussions about homosexuality as a child and I chose not to discuss these feelings with anyone. This was the beginning of my sense of isolation and aloneness that would plague me for years to come.

A significant event took place when I was a sophomore in high school. During that year I was exposed to homosexual pornography. To this day I can see myself and feel the effect that those images had on me. I couldn't stop looking at those pictures. My body ached to be touched, held, to somehow be bonded with those men in the pictures. I could not take my eyes off of those images and that event seared one thought in my mind: You are a homosexual.

As I reflect on my life, I now see that every time the enemy was offering me counterfeit life, God was ever-present to show me the truth, the real. Just as I had same-sex attractions growing up, I also had an awareness of God as demonstrated through His creation around us. There was a hunger in me to know God just as there was a hunger to know men.

I knew about God, but I didn't know Him in a personal way. I remember as a 15-year-old, crying out to Him for help in a point of anguish and desperation with my addiction to masturbation and pornography. He heard my cry. The same year I was introduced to pornography, a Franciscan priest took me to a Full Gospel Business Men's dinner where I was introduced to Jesus. My heart soared as His life and Spirit came into me. My heart recognized that this was what I was searching for. I asked Jesus to be my Savior, but I did not truly make Him Lord of my life at that time.

Dealing With God's Truth

For the next several years I was involved in the "Jesus movement" of the early '70s. In college I belonged to a Christian community house and I remember the precious fellowship, awesome times of praise and worship, and wonderful teaching. It was then that I became familiar with passages in Scripture which condemn sexual behaviors outside the context of heterosexual marriage.

In my conscience I agreed with God's truth regarding homosexual behavior. However, in order to cope with my strong feelings, I shut down my heart. By not dealing with my feelings, I placed myself in bondage to them. Knowing of no one who was walking in freedom from homosexuality, my feelings of aloneness and isolation deepened.

Because I had not made Jesus Lord of my life, willing to follow Him no matter what the cost, I walked away from Him. In 1976 1 began dating a man that I knew. Having found my "Mr. Right," I was ready to settle down into a lifelong relationship. But that "lifelong" relationship lasted only six years.

Compromise

Since I couldn't have what I thought I wanted, I compromised my life. Now I was willing to become involved with men who did not want a committed relationship. I was willing to go out to the strip clubs and, in an alcoholic blur, drown my sorrows and lost dreams. I was walking through life oblivious of my inner turmoil. I viewed other men as mere objects to satisfy my sexual appetite.

"During that year I was exposed to homosexual pornography. To this day I can see myself and feel the effect that those images had on me. I couldn't stop looking at those pictures."

As my life was consumed within the gay community in Washington, DC, I ignored the great emptiness I saw all around me. I ignored the fact that the bars were filled mainly with men under 40 years old. It was only at the strip bars and adult bookstores that I saw the "older" crowd. I overlooked the fact that any long-term relationships I did encounter were not what I considered healthy. Although some level of love existed within them, I consistently detected an emptiness as well.

Through all of this, God was still in the picture. Somehow I knew that He was waiting for me to come back to Him. By 1986 my heart had begun to yearn for Him again.

Pro-Gay Theology

I went to a gay bookstore and bought a book which stated that the Scriptures approve of homosexual behavior. I wanted to be convinced that homosexuality was acceptable and that thousands of years of interpretation and tradition was due to ignorance.

Even with this strong desire to be convinced, I remember laughing at the way the Scriptures were reinterpreted. It took no great discernment to see that justification of immoral behavior was being sought, and not God's greater purposes.

My spiritual hunger continued to grow but I became sidetracked. I began to investigate the "New Age" movement. I delved into astrology and into other areas. Then, as I was being drawn closer to the edge of darkness, God's mighty right arm reached down from on high and rescued me.

During October 1986 in San Francisco, I met a man who had a very similar background to mine. Although at that time we thought we were born as homosexuals, both of us desired a deep relationship with God. In 1987, 1 rededicated my life to the Lord. This time I wanted Jesus to truly be Lord of my life, especially over my sexuality.

Not knowing what else to do, I found a church in the yellow pages of the local phone directory. After a Sunday visit, I scheduled an appointment with one of the pastors and shared my story. I am so thankful that, although he admitted that he did not know how to counsel me, he said he loved me and wanted me to be a part of his church. God had His hand on me.

I wanted to be drawn into the heart of that church and He placed me with the prayer warriors. Several couples surrounded me with love, even though I did not share my struggle with them because of my pride and fear of rejection. Then, during a time of intense struggle in January 1988, 1 finally broke down and shared my story with one of the couples. How blessed I was when this couple just loved me, prayed for me, and did not reject me.

Two days later I went to a Christian bookstore and shared about my struggle with the owner. I purchased some literature he had and finally realized that I had not been born gay. A tremendous sense of peace flooded me. It was about 2:30 in the morning, so the only person I could call was my friend in San Francisco, where it was only 11:30 PM! Two weeks later, I heard about Regeneration, a nearby ministry to men and women struggling with unwanted homosexuality, and I began attending their support group in northern Virginia, which had just begun three months earlier.

What a joy it was to find others who were like me, searching for a way to process and understand our homosexual feelings. How remarkable to find out that so many had gone beyond "white-knuckling" the struggle.

Through the teachings I received, I came to understand some of the roots of my gender insecurity. I came to see that my homosexual attractions were rooted in a legitimate need which I had eroticized. I bonded with men sexually to fill the need for affirmation of my masculinity. I had blocked the source of that affirmation during my childhood.

Who I Am in Christ

Although understanding root issues was necessary to my process, the foundational truth that made the real difference was knowing who I am in Christ. I had a hunger for the Scriptures like never before. As I pored over the book of Romans, the Holy Spirit revealed the truth that my old nature, the old man, was not only crucified, but was dead and buried. It was no longer I who lived, but Christ who lived in me (see Romans 6).

"How blessed I was when this couple just loved me, prayed for me, and did not reject me."

I began to see that I was a new creation (2 Cor. 5:17). Neither my temptations nor feelings ultimately defined who I was as a person. The occurrence of a homosexual attraction or feeling did not mean, "I am a homosexual." I could experience temptation, but resist it and walk in freedom!

I also began to have a relationship with God as my "Abba," a word of intimacy similar to "Daddy" in the original biblical language. He was the only source of meeting my needs.

For many years I was confused about my identity, and centered it on my sexuality. Now, as a Christian, I can clearly see the truth: My relationship with God is the foundation of my identity. In the security of knowing my Heavenly Father, I never have to be confused again.

"Who Am I?" by Bob Ragan, www.Exodus-International.org, Copyright © 2003, Exodus International. All rights reserved. Used with permission.

(AP Photo/Megan Bigelow, Copyright 2004, used with permission)

Graciela Lora, 12, of Reading, Mass., a member of the Anchor Baptist Church and her brother Luis Lora,11, left, hold signs during a rally about the proposed amendment to ban same-sex marriage, during a legislative constitutional convention at the Statehouse in Boston, Wednesday, Feb. 11, 2004.

10
Free
At Last
By
Michael Babb

It was the spring of 1984. I stood at my office window, gazing out at the bleak sunless morning. A familiar cloud of depression descended upon me, the same feeling I'd had many times in recent months.

I've wanted so long to be free, I thought, my eyes filling with tears. But I'm as empty as ever. Is death the only way out?

I thought back on my childhood. My parents separated when I was four, due to Dad's excessive drinking. Their divorce came four years later. As a result, I felt inferior around my peers. They all had two parents and "normal" families, while I lived with my mother and two older sisters.

With no father, I lacked a role model for my masculine development. I began feeling very inadequate in relating to other boys. From about age five, I remember being interested in the male body. As I reached puberty, these attractions increased.

During high school and college, I didn't know anyone else with these struggles, and I never acted on my same-sex desires. I would have killed myself if anyone had even suspected this hidden side of my life.

I felt some attraction to women, and fell in love with a classmate whom I married. After nine months, however, my wife was killed in a car accident. She died without ever knowing about my secret battle.

Two other close relatives died over the next three years. I started wishing that I could die, too. Maybe I'll be next, I told myself. Then I won't have to live with this horrible struggle anymore.

The happiest time of my life occurred after I accepted Jesus as my Savior in 1974. Growing up in a legalistic denomination, I had thought that if you lived right, you were automatically a Christian. Then several of my friends joined the Jesus People movement, and started talking about Jesus Christ all the time. One night alone in my apartment, I prayed a simple prayer: "Lord, if I don't know You yet, I really want to. I want a better life. I want help."

My life started changing after that prayer. I quit swearing and smoking marijuana. As I read the Bible, I experienced a deep joy. For the first time in my life, I knew God really loved me. My homosexual struggles subsided, and finally I felt some of the freedom which I desperately wanted. This healing process continued for several years.

During this time, I started attending evening classes at a nearby Bible college. One night another student named Beth shared her testimony, and the Lord spoke to my heart: "You're going to marry her." Beth and I knew each other casually, but our relationship quickly deepened after that night. We were married four months later.

I was a husband again, and my homosexual feelings decreased a lot. But the roots of my struggle were still unresolved. Then I started going through typical mid-life feelings, especially after two job changes. At age

35, I saw my body getting older and began fantasizing about sex with younger men.

I became strongly attracted to a business associate, and we began spending time together almost every evening. Our relationship turned into an emotional dependency, then became sexual. Soon I was ready to leave my wife, my job and my God for this man. I knew in my heart what I was doing was wrong, but I had no strength to stop it.

My guilt turned to depression. I knew my marriage was falling apart. The more time I spent with my friend, the less I wanted to be with Beth. One night she received an anonymous phone call. "Your husband is seeing someone else," the person said, then hung up.

Later Beth confronted me, but I denied everything. "I'm just working late," I lied, my stomach churning. I was consumed with frustration. My once-happy marriage was now a roadblock to my raging desires for the gay world.

"I've wanted so long to be free, I thought, my eyes filling with tears. But I'm as empty as ever. Is death the only way out?"

Looking out the window that bleak spring day in 1984, I realized that the very thing which I had craved all those years had let me down. Finally I'm in love with another man, I told myself, and I wish I were dead!

Then came a phone call that changed my life. Julie, the wife of a former pastor, telephoned me from Boston. Knowing I was depressed, she had prayed diligently for me. Through the Holy Spirit, God revealed to her specific details of my struggles.

"I have two words for you," she told me. "Homosexuality--and suicide."

"You're right," I admitted, feeling a huge relief that my hidden sins were finally coming out into the open. Julie let me know that, no matter what happened, she still loved me. "I'll always be here for you," she said.

After I hung up the phone, Beth walked into the room. "Do you want to tell me what that was all about?" she asked.

"Well, you know we have just a shell of a marriage," I began. "It's a weak relationship, not even a friendship..." Then I uttered two simple words that had been locked inside me for years: "I'm gay."

I told Beth what I'd been going through, and the next evening we had a long talk. "Do you love me?" she asked. "Do you love him more than me? If you want him, then go. If you don't, I'm here to work this through with you." As she spoke, I realized that my great fear of rejection was unfounded. My deepest secret was coming out, and the people closest to me were responding in love.

Immediately God began intervening in my life. I had to face my friend almost every day at work, but then a job offer came from Oklahoma city, 150 miles south. Both my wife and I felt the separation and new surroundings would be ideal. We put our house on the market, and I moved to Oklahoma.

After I'd been at my new job for six months, I went on vacation with my family. At a friend's house, I found the testimony of a former homosexual, Sy Rogers. I locked myself in the bathroom and read the tract three times! After vacation, I wrote to Sy. He wrote back a beautiful letter, giving me some scriptures and encouragement. We started writing back and forth, and he told me about The First Stone, a local ex-gay ministry in Oklahoma City.

Several months later, I went for a one-on-one session with a counselor, and knew immediately that this ministry was for me. I felt such love, acceptance and understanding, which I desperately needed.

I learned about the vital importance of a moment-by-moment relationship with Jesus, which would bring peace and joy to my life. God showed me that I needed to know Him intimately--not just intellectually. I realized that, in the years since I'd become a Christian, I had learned a lot about God, but I didn't really know Him. I knew about homosexual abstinence, but not about healing from homosexuality.

God showed me that nothing would come upon me that I couldn't handle, that He would provide a way out (see 1 Cor. 10:13). Homosexual temptations would come, that was certain. But, when they came, I could learn from them; God would use even temptation for my good.

I also learned how to control my lustful thoughts, by submitting them to Jesus through prayer. When my eyes wandered, I would stop and begin making right choices, not allowing my emotions to go wild with lust. Slowly I learned the meaning of "taking up your cross" and following Jesus (Matt. 16:24), denying the old desires of my flesh. Sometimes I didn't want to obey Christ. I fell into old habits, but I got up and kept going.

After a year-and-a-half, our house in Kansas was still unsold. I received another job offer back in Wichita, and the apartment where I was living in Oklahoma became unavailable.

God gave me a strong impression: "Go back to Wichita and begin a ministry to homosexuals." By the end of December 1986, I was back home in Kansas. Four months later, our first group meeting occurred--and we have been going strong ever since.

"Homosexual temptations would come, that was certain. But, when they came, I could learn from them; God would use even temptation for my good."

My own healing continues. God has brought me to the point where I no longer see myself as "gay." Although I experience homosexual desires from time to time, they don't control me. Now I look forward to each day with joyful anticipation, not with a tight emotional knot down inside. After years of struggle, I'm walking in His freedom--at last.

"Free at Last" by Michael Babb, www.Exodus-International.org. Copyright © *2003, Exodus International. All rights reserved. Used with permission.*

(AP Photo/Chitose Suzuki, Copyright 2004, used with permission)

Julie Goodridge, left, and her partner Hillary, right, who were the plaintiffs in the Massachusetts gay marriage lawsuit, speak to reporters following a news conference in Boston, Wednesday, Feb. 4, 2004 to discuss an advisory opinion issued by the Massachusetts Supreme Judicial Court. The court issued the opinion that only full, equal marriage rights for gay couples, rather than civil unions, would meet the edict of its November 2003 decision.

I seemed I had it all - my homosexual lifestyle and love, without the drugs, alcohol and bulimia, a great job, beautiful home, and great homosexual friends. I attended church faithfully every week - and felt I had it all. But God wasn't done with me yet - in fact, He had just started.

"Things only grew worse and for a period of 6 years I declined morally, mentally and physically."

My doorbell rang, and it was my friend Kathy, a friend for years who had seen me through the good and bad times of my life - and she had a Bible in her hand, and asked if she could come in. She had told me she left her religious background and became a Christian. She told me how Jesus changed her life, and how according to the Bible homosexuality was wrong - it was a sin and an abomination in God's eyes - how according to the Bible I was not "born that way" -- and that Jesus could set me free - today. I listened intently, and something inside of me told me she was right. I told her I would take the Bible and she left. That day, the Word of God cut right through me - I saw my homosexuality for the first time as God saw it - *as sin*. Anytime something would happen between me and my partner sexually, I found myself praying for forgiveness to God on my bathroom floor. God was tugging at my heart strings, and I knew it.

The tugging was so hard and clear, I left my partner, my job, my family - everything and headed off to Provincetown, MA - a homosexual subculture - to live for a summer, to see if I could reconcile this pull between being a homosexual and a Christian. Did I have to choose one or the other, or could I be both at the same time in God's eyes?

Well, in that summer of 1991 God opened my eyes to the truth and perverseness of the homosexual lifestyle. I saw it all in full swing, in all its glory - transsexuals, transvestites, sadomasochists - men and women doing things one would never even imagine.

After 5 months in Provincetown, I returned home to my partner asking for forgiveness for leaving him - I was sorry and I was going to put this "Christian" business aside. After only 4 short months at home in his house, by myself while wrapping Christmas presents, I happened to flip through radio stations and came across a Christian one. A man was singing a song and I heard the lyrics about "men marching for their right to sin". I knew exactly what the song was talking about - *it was talking about me*. I may have put God on the back burner - but He was still chasing after me.

On New Year's eve I attended a homosexual party with my partner, and for the first time ever in my life - I felt "dirty." I hated myself. I hated my lifestyle. But I just couldn't break free.

I called my friend Kathy on the telephone, and told her I was going to move back to Provincetown, MA for good and completely give myself over to the homosexual lifestyle. I felt as if I lost my soul - I was crying out for help - and that's when Jesus Christ stepped in.

"...God opened my eyes to the truth and perverseness of the homosexual lifestyle."

She read to me from the Bible, from the book of Romans, how God will "call" you - and if He keeps calling you, and you hear, yet harden your heart, it may come to a point where He will make you a "reprobate" in His sight and give you completely over to your sin, and allow you to believe "the lie." At that point, according to the Bible, you have basically sealed your destiny away from Him forever.

It scared me so much, I asked her what I needed to do, and she told me right now to pray to Jesus - ask Him to deliver me from the homosexuality - and Him to forgive me for my sins, and to come into my heart and life, be my Lord and Saviour, and to take control. At that moment, I did and physically felt the peace of God upon me. That day in January of 1992, on the telephone, I asked Jesus to come into my heart - and He set me free. That day God changed my life forever and I will be eternally grateful to Him for what He did. Within 2 weeks of that time I moved out of my partner's home and was on my way and walk with Jesus Christ.

Within 2 months of accepting Jesus Christ as my Savior, I knew deep down I had to deal with the root cause of my homosexuality in order to move on with my life. For me, it was a broken relationship with my father.

For years, I only desired one thing: my father's love. I knew as Jesus had forgiven me for all of my sins - past, present and future - I now needed to extend that forgiveness that I received - to my father. After confronting him one day, pouring out my heart and really talking for the very first time -- our broken relationship was reconciled. Forgiveness was extended and the chains that bound me for years were unshackled.

Today, my father and I have a wonderful relationship. I love my dad and I know he loves me. I realized for all of those years, I was vainly looking for the love of my father in the arms of other men. Today, the search is over: *I have the real thing.*

I must say, it is incredible how my journey has been. Within that first year, I was engaged to a beautiful Christian woman, Irene, who knew me as a homosexual, and was praying for me for years. We were married on June 13, 1993. Today, over ten years later -- and very happily married -- God has blessed us with two other miracles - my beautiful daughter Chloe Catherine who is 5 years old, and my son Blake Stephen, 3 years old, born on Chloe's birthday. Chloe's middle name is in dedication to my friend Kathy who never gave up on me - a vessel of God, who He used to change my destiny forever.

I asked Jesus to come into my heart - and He set me free. That day God changed my life forever and I will be eternally grateful to Him for what He did.

Today life is wonderful - I am free, and it is all because of Jesus Christ and His love for me. Jesus is the answer for all of our needs, no matter what they are. You may be, know or live with a homosexual, a drug addict, or an alcoholic. Understand - God loves the sinner - He just hates the sin.

Remember, with God, nothing is impossible - believe me, I know. I do believe in miracles - I believe in miracles, for I've seen a soul set free... for that lost soul was *me*.

"God's Amazing Grace" by Stephen Bennett, Copyright © 2001-2004, Stephen Bennett Ministries, All rights reserved. Used with permission.

(AP Photo/Patricia McDonnell, Copyright 2004, used with permission)

Naomi Robertson, center, of Boston joins fellow church members in song
Thursday morning, March 11, 2004 outside the Statehouse in Boston, calling on
the state legislature to vote against legalizing same-sex marriage.

12
Finally Finding Real Love

By

Star Burch

I'll admit that I had been "feeling" females on and off for years since I was about age 8, maybe younger. Every couple of years a female would come around and tempt me. Being the person that I was, I gave in. With age and maturity I grew smarter, however, not strong enough to resist the temptation of the enemy. I had a relationship with God but did not really know what it really meant. I was 11 years old having conversations with God just like I would with anyone else. My whole existence was based on a relationship that I didn't quite understand. I wasn't saved until after my 12th birthday. I remember the prayer that changed my life. I prayed that I could do something awesome for GOD to show him I loved him. I didn't know exactly what I was praying for and I didn't know how much that 'lil prayer would change my life but it did. That prayer has stayed with me even till this day. Even in the midst of my sins God never forgot about me. I soon began to experience things that caused me to know who this Jesus was beyond a shadow of a doubt. I grew up in a Christian home and attended a Pentecostal/holiness church all the time.

At first, I didn't live a consistent life with Christ. After a couple of years of living for the Lord I fell off. I began listening to another female who started me on a deep, downward spiral. I was 17 years old at the time I decided I couldn't fight my lesbian desires anymore. I finally gave in and officially admitted that I was a homosexual. It all seems so weird to me now. Some things I wouldn't do, so how gay could I have really been? God revealed to me that I only wanted to be with women because I needed a mother figure. My girlfriend became everything to me, a mother, sister, best friend...EVERYTHING. One day God revealed to me what she really was doing for me. When I was sick my lover took care of me, when I needed a perm, needed my scalp greased...she would even clean the plaque off my teeth (I'm just telling the truth)! God also revealed to me what I was doing for her. I helped her to become an independent woman, however, all the baggage that I brought into our relationship became hers too. What's worse, as our relationship developed, I (yes me) became abusive, first verbally and then physically. I knew I needed to take a step back. We went to school together and served together with *Students for Christ*. If you would have told us that we would have "hooked up" and fell in love we would of laughed at you. How could we end up in a gay relationship?

I finally reached my lowest point. One day I found myself laying in a bathtub, half conscience and half naked. I wasn't quite sure where I was but my girlfriend was right by my side, like a mother. I had tried to commit suicide over an ex-lover, who could of cared less if I lived or died. I was hysterical. I used to be so hooked on this woman it was scary. I laid there crying out, calling out her name, saying over and over "why didn't she love me?" I screamed her name so loud to the point where my girlfriend left the room and began to cry herself. This went on until I became unconscious again. That night I should have died, however, God was good to me.

I decided I to go out to a club and have a good time to forget about her. I was broken and sin had its hands around my throat. I had a very low tolerance for alcohol but I tried to drown myself in Seagram's gin. I blacked out before I even made it to the club.

"I finally gave in and officially admitted that I was a homosexual."

My relationships were crumbling all around me. Another ex-lover was in a car accident in another state. God gave me a revelation that she had the accident because of me. My disobedience to God almost cost her life. When you're chosen by God, anything that separates you from GOD will be moved out of the way by any means necessary.

Would you like to know what caused me to change?

I had a praying grandmother, mother, and many friends who lifted me up before God in madd prayer, but what really made the difference was ME. I wanted to change, I needed to change, I had to change. The devil thought he had me all the way, but one thing happened the devil didn't realize. God had his hands on me. The devil didn't know my love for God became stronger then anything he could tempt me with in this world. I was tired of being depressed, unhappy and wanting to die. I wanted out. The woman whose love I so craved could no longer penetrate my heart. Her love wasn't good enough for me anymore. I needed the love of Jesus to fill the emptiness in my life. I realized nothing would compare to Jesus' love when he died on the cross for me.

This is not the *end* of my testimony but just the *beginning.* Many of the things that happened in my life worked together to create who I am today. Although, I've changed, changed, and changed some more, the one thing that has never changed was God. He has never left me nor forsaken me. Even when I tried to forget about God and deny Him he still took care of me. I can't count how many times I should have died, but the mercy and grace of God held me close to him. I can't count how many times in the past the devil either tried to or did trick me but GOD was always right there pulling at my heart strings saying "hey kid-o I love u, come back."

69

Every time life gets hard I envision GOD on his thrown in Heaven with his hand reached out towards me saying "let me hold you now." Now, church has a new meaning to me. It's not just *going to* church, it's how I get fortified. I cast all of my cares on Him.

Since I gave Jesus control of my life IT FEELS SO GOOD! He has been my keeper (Jude 24), so I thank him for a clean life. Have I been tested? LORD KNOWS YES! But GOD has been faithful. I`m not perfect and I make mistakes but I realize Jesus is my help and although I fall I can still get up. I`ve gained the gift of GOODBYE. I'm learning to let the women of my past go so I can grow. Deliverance is a process so I'm letting God completely heal the wounds of the past. Some days it hurts more then others and I catch myself slipping emotionally, but I press on. This is what living the new, abundant life in Christ is all about!

"Even when I tried to forget about God and deny Him he still took care of me."

I am CRUNK, EXCITED, AND ON FIRE FOR GOD! I am Loving Jesus everyday. GOD has brought me so far from where I used to be. I'm peaceful, I have joy, and I love people! I care and I want my testimony minister to those that want to be blessed by GOD. He can loose the bonds of wickedness from anyone just like he did for me and others who were caught in the "lifestyle." We are living, breathing testimonies that JESUS does still SAVE. Life after lesbianism is so much different. No longer am I on the outside looking in, I'm now on the inside seeing what GOD can do for myself. Awesome! All I can say is Awesome. I`ve seen him do great things and in Jesus I've finally found the real love that I have always wanted.

"Finally Finding Real Love" by Natashia D. Burch, Copyright © 2003. All rights reserved. Used with permission.

13

Deliverance from Lesbianism

By

Mignon K. Middleton

My first exposure to lesbianism was in the tenth grade. In my mind I knew that homosexuality existed, but I had never really been exposed to it until then. Their names were, well, lets call them Nina & Terri. Terri was an extremely intriguing 'butch' female who was a lesbian. Nina was her attractive feminine girlfriend. I would see them in the hallways engaging in the type of exchanges that took place in all normal relationships. I would see Terri carrying Nina's bags for her. I would even see them holding hands, hugging and kissing in the hallways, like in any normal relationship. Only this relationship wasn't normal in my world. This was something new to me. Something new that seemed to connect with something inside of me. It resonated in my soul as the answer to a question that I had been trying to solve for so very long. This relationship between them wasn't normal, but in my eyes it was superior to what I had deemed to be normal up until this point.

I observed them from a distance, in admiration, as well as in total terror due to the uncertainty of what my pre-occupation was implying. I automatically began verbally denouncing homosexuality and voiced my disgust and puzzlement about their way of life. Being a 'Christian', I knew that homosexuality was not part of God's plan for us. So I did my best to convince myself as well as the people around me that it was sin and that it was wrong.

I succeeded in my state of denial until my eleventh grade year. I silently battled with thoughts and visions, doubts and confusion about my sexuality and about God. I finally shared my struggle with my best friend, and she shared with me that she had been having the same struggle. We both knew, but we weren't sure, so we didn't want to risk telling each other something that personal for fear of rejection.

Like many others, I tried to resolve my dilemma by praying and going to church. One reason was because I knew that it wasn't a part of God's will for me to live my life as a lesbian. Another reason was because I didn't want to be different. I didn't want this curse. I cried out to God to take the desires and tormenting thoughts away from me. But nothing seemed to change.

On the other hand, I also felt like I would be much happier if I stopped trying to resist this path that seemed to have inevitably chosen me. If I would just go with the flow, and let whatever happens, just happen. God would still love me right? If He wanted me to be different, then He would change me, right? And He didn't seem to be trying to change me, so maybe I needed to stop trying to change myself. So eventually I did.

Earlier I stated, " It resonated in my soul as the answer to the question that I had been trying to solve for so very long." What was this question that seemed to plague me? There were actually many questions: Why do

16

Living a Life of Change and Promise

By

Darryl L. Foster

The night was falling fast in Columbus, Georgia and I was sinking deeper in the quicksand of sin, sinking to rise no more. Somehow in my heart I knew I was going down for the last time and there would be no recovery. Years and years as a homosexual man had burned away all of my sensitivities. The thoughts of suicide had seeded themselves and were maturing quickly. I hated my life and what I had become. I saw no way out except that my life would adn should end. Death seemed to be a good thing, because I no longer wanted to look at myself go through the motions of life with no hope for change.

I don't know what made me turn on the television that night. I really didn't want to look at it. It was reactionary, perhaps a habit that I had become so accustomed to that I simply did what I had always done when I was tired and depressed. Yet, looking back I can believe that it was time. A point in destiny. A date to meet the man whose passion for me caused him to endure the terrible brutality heaped upon him.

When the TV screen came into focus and my eyes immediately fell upon a troubling scene. It was brutal to me. Thousands of people lined a stone road which had an increasing incline as it wound its way through the city. The people, it appeared were in a frenzy. An evil frame of mind which one can only imagine the extent of. But I also saw the object of their evil desires. It was a lonely figure coming slowly up the arduous road. As I watched alarmed, he approached me under a barrage of insults. Some screamed at him. Others threw rocks at him. Still others reached out as it they wanted to take him and tear him to shreds with their bare hands. But still he moved on. And I continued to watch, mesmerized.

He was not alone. On his back he struggled under a heavy wooden cross. It was twice his body size. One would think that to see such suffering, people would be compassionate. Not this crowd, the cross seemed to enrage them the more. Still he struggled on, never saying a word, never lifting his eyes. In my intellect I didn't know who he was. It had been so long since I'd thought about God or church or Jesus that I drew blanks as to his identity. But even in my own pain and the desire to end my life, I became engrossed in his dilemma. I heard my mind ask a single, silent, fearful question. What did he do to make these people hate him so much?

Then a strange then happened. The "scene" froze. Everyone and everything. Nothing moved except him. That was when it struck home. As I looked, his eyes rose up to meet mine. I saw him and it was like looking into the eyes of someone who has always known you. The blood from a crown of thorns pressed hastily into his head trickled down different parts of his face. He said to me, "I did all of this just for you." Then he lowered his head again and continued on up the hill with his cross, on his way to PROVE what he had just said.

When I came to myself I looked again at the crowd. This time I recognized a familiar face: it was my own. I also realized it was Jesus who has spoken to me.

I began to sob and weep. I couldn't believe that he could or would love me after all that I had done. What did his words mean? Did he really love me enough to suffer through the insanity of man and the affliction of God? He did. He truly did.

Eventually, in the same room I had carried on numerous male sexual affairs, I fell on my face before this Man. I asked him to forgive me and cleanse me of my sin and the years of rebellion. During the time I lay there it seemed the heavens were opened and the glory of God came in. I got up knowing that no matter what happened, I would always love him and I knew that he would always love me. In a word, I was changed. Yes, now I was free, but it hadn't always been that way.

"The thoughts of suicide had seeded themselves and were maturing quickly. I hated my life and what I had become."

When I looked at myself as a young boy in the mirror, all I could see was a weak, timid boy full of fear, self-loathing and pain. I couldn't relate to other boys my age except in one way. And that was a deep dark secret I hoped no one would ever discover.

I was born into a church family. In the African American religious tradition, the generations of family involved in the church was a badge of honor. Church was a place where, in spite of the hardships faced by outside pressures--especially racism--black people felt special.

Unfortunately, I didn't meet my father until I was seven years old. He gave my brother and me a few dollars and left again; I did not see him again for another six years. By this time, I was full of anger and hatred at his uncaring abandonment.

"Do we call him 'Daddy'?" my little brother asked.

"No, we'll just call him 'sir'," I replied. I was determined to sound as cold as possible. When we saw my father this time, he rubbed our heads and offered us a few dollars. This time, I refused his money; I hated him so much that I couldn't have cared if he had offered us a thousand dollars.

The lack of having a father around took a heavy toll on me; I developed a deep longing for a man to hold me in his arms and tell me he loved me. I struggled with feelings of rejection caused in part my father's unexplained absence. I had no confidence in my masculinity or in my abilities as a male among other males. I endured the rejection and ridicule of other boys my age, while at the same time developing unwanted emotional and physical attractions to them. I wasn't even aware of my tendency to sexualize relationships with other males until I was about 11.

Even though I grew up in the "sanctified" church and loved going to church, I struggled constantly with homosexual thoughts. Amid the "shouting and dancing so characteristic of our black worship experience, I hid my struggle as best I could. Our church believed strongly in deliverance. That is to say whatever your problem was, someone could lay hands on you and pray--and the problem would be solved. I desperately wanted my homosexual desires to just disappear. That was my fantasy. That one day they would all just go away.

But even with all the preaching about deliverance, I was left confused. While they said God could do anything, it seemed not to apply to homosexuality. Homosexuality in the black church could only be whispered about in private.

These circumstances made me a magnet for manipulation so at the age of 13 an older boy inmy church sexually molested me. The feelings in my heart became a vortex of battling conflicts. I hated his touch and I longed for his touch. I hated liking his attention and I hated not having his attention.

Over the next three years, I was forced to bear "Ray's" relentless obsession with me. Thankfully, we never had sex. When I finally left the church in disgust, I left home and plunged headlong into the gay lifestyle. The sight of men dancing with each other and publicly kissing made me feel so good. I felt like I was finally in a place where I belonged.

In 1980, my first year of college, I dove headlong into homosexuality and all it had to offer. I was new on the gay scene; soon everyone was asking who I was and who I was dating. I went to house parties, orgies, got hooked on "poppers" and started drinking. I was like a kid in a candy store with no parents around!

In 1982, I hid my homosexuality so I could join the Army. I traveled all over the world and everywhere I could always find another man to have sex with. I went through periods of deep depression, when I felt so lonely I wanted to die. When I came out of my depression, I had to have sex to make me feel powerful and secure. I developed a hard attitude toward others, even my lovers. People existed to give me pleasure; when I was finished, I simply discarded them.

At the height of my life as a gay man I felt invincible! No one could stop me, not even God. "I don't care if I go to hell!" I told God when I felt convicted about my sexuality. But I was still unhappy and unfulfilled. Thoughts tormented me that I now believe came from satan: You can find sex partners anytime you want, but none of them love you. It was an attempt to push me further along the path of self destruction. After years of homosexual sex in all its devaluing forms, I still felt unloved and worthless.

"I hid my homosexuality so I could join the Army. I traveled all over the world and everywhere I could always find another man to have sex with."

That was over 14 years ago. Of course, there were many issues to confront as I started down the road to total healing. Healing was and is a process that I embrace with all my heart. God directed me to a church, where I stayed for five years, rising to become second assistant pastor.

I was moving away from the residual issues of anger, hatred, and improper sexual passions. Yet I still had to deal with new challenges. Would I be accepted in the church? Would the men sense my homosexual past? Was I really free?

Over the next few years, God proved his faithfulness by allowing me to build healthy relationships with godly men who loved me without prejudice. They didn't realize it, but God was using them to heal me of feelings of self-worthlessness.

Eventually, I met a young woman who had begun attending the same church and we became friends. Over the next year, God confirmed in many ways that we belonged together. My passions changed and I knew God had created me to love a woman, not a man. Before I proposed to Dee, I told her about my past. "Honey" she responded, "if God has forgiven you, so do I." We were married and began our life together.

Today, almost 12 years later that woman, Dee is still my wife, and is still the most beautiful woman in the world. She is the mother of my four children and the love of my life.

God has greatly used my wife to work miracles in my healing process. She was instrumental in hearing his voice for me to take my testimony public so that others could hear and be set free.

Most of all, Jesus assured me that he would "never leave me nor forsake me" (Heb. 13:5). It hasn't been an easy journey but, because of God's love, power and faithfulness, I am and will continue to be a whole man. My deepest desires for love and belonging have been met, through Jesus Christ and his family, the Church.

Because of the grace and power of the Lord Jesus, I'm no longer the broken, hate-driven homosexual man I used to be. I live for and enjoy my life serving the Lord Jesus, raising my children, loving my wife and leading the congregation God has given me the favor to lead. These are the fruits of change. A promise that only be fulfilled in a life submitted to God.

"Living a Life of Change and Promise" by Pastor Darryl L. Foster, Adapted from the book "Touching A Dead Man: One man's explosive story of deliverance from homosexuality," Copyright © 2002, used with permission.

(AP Photo/Michael Dwyer, Copyright 2004, used with permission)

Ruben Israel of Los Angeles, right, confronts opponents of the same-sex marriage amendment to the Massachusetts constitution outside the Statehouse in Boston, Thursday, March 11, 2004.

17

I Overcame

By

Fred L. Phelps

My testimony begins 12 years ago when I first came to Atlanta, Ga. in 1992: The Lord spoke to me and urged me to move from Kentucky to Atlanta. At the time I thought it was just for a better opportunity regarding my job. Little did I know the Lord wanted to do a work outside of the confines of my comfort zones and religious experiences. I came to Atlanta as single man, an ordained minister of the gospel and a recent college graduate with a life that was broken and slowly being sifted by the enemy.

I knew in my heart that my lifestyle was wrong. I struggled with homosexuality and had distorted views of God and myself. I knew God loved me but never really trusted Him as Father and deliverer. I was even shaky about him really being Savior. I was going through the motions filled with pain, disgust and condemnation. My life was like a whirlwind, moving quickly but never arriving at a place of surrender.

The Leadership at the Church I attend referred me to a support group called Katupau: (Now Resurrection Life Ministries) for men who struggled with sexual additions, namely homosexuality. I received one on one counseling and attended a small group, where I began to truly deal with sexual abuse, unresolved anger, bitterness, poor self-image and un-forgiveness. My ears were truly opened to the voice of God during this time period in my life and the Lord affirmed me as His son.

I grew up in a small town in Kentucky: born out of wedlock and the first and only male child of my parents. I lived ashamed of the poverty and dysfunctional lifestyle my family walked in. I was a middle child of 3 and felt I never truly fit in. We lived on welfare until my mother got a steady job and left my father. My father was in and out of prison since he was 15 years old: He lived with us from the time I was 3 until I was about 9 or 10 yrs old. He was an alcoholic and was the youngest of 5 children. He was molested by his brothers and also was violated in prison. He in turn molested me.

I knew that my parents loved me but they were not very touchy or affectionate people, except on certain occasions. My relationship with them was dysfunctional. My father was abusive toward my mother and she would always call me to the rescue: I grew up quickly in our household, (man of the house role) I was my mother's confidant and warrior in a sense when my father wasn't there. My mother never violated me sexually, but I was put in adult roles as a child. My mom did the best she knew to do in raising us and I respect her and love her for it, however, there were some issues I had to forgive her for in our relationship.

My father began molesting me at the age of 3 or 4 I believe: It started out as a game and our little secrete: I played along, not truly understanding what was happening: When I went into the first grade the game changed and so did the plays: It turned into rape and the fear as well as hate for my father grew daily toward him: I didn't want him in our house nor in my life: The abuse he showed toward me and my mother was traumatic and devastating: I use to cry hysterically when they would argue or physically fight: I was terrified and at times would grow weak: To this day I still have to process my emotions in a way that is healthy without doing something I will regret or just shut down emotionally. When being confronted I have to fight and discern the true heart of the confronter. When arguing at times, I have to fight through emotions under the realization that I do have a voice to and don't have to submit to the sudden fear and rage that bound me as a child. This has shown the root of my behavior leading back to my parents and that fearful child who just wanted love and affirmation.

"I knew in my heart that my lifestyle was wrong. I struggled with homosexuality and had distorted views of God and myself."

One of the significant wounds that led to the sin pattern in my life was the wound of my father: The violation of trust with men and male affirmation: As a result I yielded toward the feminine: It was safe to be with women and not be judged at least openly. I was not pressured to do the 'man thing'. I couldn't live up to society's view of masculinity, I wasn't athletic enough, I wasn't smooth talking enough nor hard enough. The bottom line was I wasn't healed enough. I would seek affirmation in various sexual encounters with men. The sexual acts I had with men, the struggle with pornography and masturbation was a way I would numb out pain, feel a sense of acceptance and unfortunately love. I didn't really trust or even love God as I thought, because he wanted to touch me in places, I didn't want to be touched in. In other words, surrendering my heart meant giving all and I didn't want to do that and be hurt at the same time. Therefore, I couldn't be satisfied with His love alone and I didn't really know what love was. I never committed myself to one person because that would mean falling in love so to speak and that I was not going to do. I couldn't relate to women as a love interest because most of my life I had been with men. I had a few girl friends to keep up an image. As I started to let the Lord touch me in those broken place, it was becoming even harder to continue sexual encounters with men, because the conviction and condemnation that caused me to be miserable. I didn't know who I truly was under the mask of all the pain and brokenness I had lived in so long. Therefore my relational skills were very weak and timid: I needed the Lord to really do a work in my heart.

I went to the counselor at Resurrection Life and he referred me to another part of the ministry that did a deeper work. I was referred to a discipleship program called Living Waters: It was what the doctor ordered for my life at that time. I was settling in the Church I was attending: becoming more involved, developing more relationships: God had allowed me to face my past with my father and forgive him as well be forgiven before my father died. Walking more and more in the early part of my healing and restoration, for the first time I saw a glimmer of hope for myself yet there was more work to be done.

The 26 weeks at Living waters opened up doors of wounds and brokenness that need to be mended and Christ did that. I began to see some of the root causes to the perverted motives I had carried in my heart. I began to see where boundaries where broken in my life and needed to be rebuilt in a healthy way. I began to accept "my true self" in God's image as his handy work. I saw the grace of God to aid me in relating in healthy ways to men without feeling intimidated or less than or that I had to have sex with them. At the same time I began to relate with women in a way that was healthy as well. With the wound of my mother, I always felt I owed women something so I was the crutch, the one who didn't want to cause any problems, always be one to bring peace. Living waters helped me to see the feminine and the masculine in the image of Christ, the good of them both and the balance that is so greatly needed.

Presently at the Church I attend, we have weekend-encounters that are used as an instrument to engage greater deliverance in the lives of new as well as seasoned believers. It's a process that is encompassed our Corporate vision for our Church to "Win souls and Make disciples" The encounter weekend is a weekend with God and trusted believers that guides one greater healing at the cross of Christ. Issues that need the hand of God are addressed in this weekend: Issues of Rejection, fear, addictions, un-forgiveness, generational curses, and sexual sins: All these and more are addressed at the encounter at the cross. This has brought even greater healing in my life as well: It reiterates the fullness of Christ at the cross that I've experienced at Living Waters. They both go hand in hand for those who struggle sexually outside the confines of marriage.

As God has and is still healing me, He brought a wonderful woman in my life. We were married June 14, 2003: It has truly been an eye opener for me to see still how much I need God's love and healing in my heart and in some areas that I really never paid attention.... i.e..... just how selfish I can be, or prideful and a great need to be delivered from a performance lifestyle. I'm learning about vulnerability, while I fear it at times can be my savior in a sense: Opening up to my wife and speaking without shame as it relates to my past or even present struggles creates such an atmosphere of freedom, acceptance and love because of the God in my wife and the transparency we must walk in. I'm grateful for the grace God in allowing me to see these things though painful they are at times, it's an opportunity of growth. I'm amazed to see how God unites 2 people and deals with both hearts to make them one. I love my wife and learning to love her in spite of what I feel and see at times in my wife as well as myself. We have a ways to go but I'm enjoying the journey.

"Issues that need the hand of God are addressed in this weekend: Issues of Rejection, fear, addictions, un-forgiveness, generational curses, and sexual sins: All these and more are addressed at the encounter at the cross."

Presently I'm back to Living Waters this time as small group leader and see some things I missed: (It's been a continual healing for me still even in my sexuality) My wife is going through as a participant initially to support me, but I've seen God do a work in her life to the point where she feels she a part of Living Waters ministry for life as I do.

"I Overcame" by Fred L. Phelps, Copyright © 2004, Used with permission.

(AP Photo/Charles Krupa, Copyright 2004, used with permission)

Hillary and her partner, Julie Goodridge, left, the lead plaintiffs in the
Massachusetts gay marriage lawsuit, fill out their marriage license application,
with Boston Mayor Tom Menino looking over their shoulder, at Boston City Hall in
Boston, Monday May 17, 2004.

18

From Darkness to a Life Beyond Imagination

By

Ron Elmore

My soul delights to praise Him who has called me out of the darkness of homosexuality into His marvelous light.

My father died of cancer three months after I was born. Within two years of his death creditors auctioned most of his assets, and our family home was destroyed by a fire. With nine mouths to feed and no husband, Mother had to place us in an orphanage. Before my twin brother and I were six years old, she began preparing us for the transition into the Children's Home that my older siblings had already made. Yet this was not what I wanted. I wanted her! Even as she painted a picture of playmates and close brotherhood, I began to be filled with fear of her absence.

Arriving at the home, my brother and I were incorporated with the younger boys and forbidden to enter the area which housed our older brothers. Child care at the home was regimented and strict. Discipline came to me through anyone who was older than I was. I heard only criticism and questioning. I began to have nightmares. I dreamed of calling out to my Mom, frustrated that she could not find me. I could hear her calling my name. But I could not respond to her. Unknown to anyone, I had already been sexually abused several times by a male family friend.

I hurt from the abandonment of my Mom, the rejection of my brothers and others, and the ongoing sexual abuse that had become a pattern in my life. Being molested by older boys, summer camp counselors, and even pastors reinforced the confusion and pain. I struggled terribly because the very people who were to be my protectors abused me. There seemed to be this shameful, overpowering force pulling me into inappropriate relationships with other boys. My boundaries of physical touch had been broken and sexualized at an early age. I did not understand boundaries or what was happening to me physically.

At fifteen, I felt a strong calling to the ministry. I sought and received permission to share publicly in the campus church about my life with Christ. The Lord used that evening. Children of all ages came and filled the altar in surrender to His call. But Satan came to me and spoke a lie: "If anyone knew what you have been doing with other boys, no one would ever allow you to stand in a pulpit and tell others about Jesus Christ. Who do you think you are?" Running in shame and condemnation, I fled out the back door of the choir room, hid in the garden and vowed, "I will never stand in front of anyone again to tell them about Jesus." At that moment, I attempted to reject Christ.

When I left the orphanage in March of 1975, I was hurting and sexually confused. At first I stayed with my mother while I finished my junior year of high-school. At the end of that year, my sister and her pastor persuaded me to move to a Christian college in Virginia to finish high school and perhaps take some college courses.

During summer break, I walked blindly into a gay club at the beach. With the blaring disco songs of a popular vocalist, I began a very long journey in the homosexual lifestyle.

I believed I had finally found male acceptance through homosexual contact. Shortly afterwards, I joined the Air Force at the urging of my mother. Becoming more and more ambivalent to God, I found my place in the gay nightclubs near the city where I lived. For two years, everything was great with an over abundance of everything I thought I wanted. Then I endured two abusive long term relationships. Each relationship brought me deeper into the homosexual subculture. During those years of involvement I developed a deep suspicion of others mixed with anger and lust. I spiraled deeper and deeper into drugs, alcohol, and pornography. In my anxiety, I frequented the bars, homosexual establishments and adult bookstores. Even as the cavern in my soul grew bigger my Spirit testified to me that I was in rebellion.

"Unknown to anyone, I had already been sexually abused several times by a male family friend."

In 1987, a co-worker who knew I was an active homosexual and could tell I had been using drugs, confronted me. "Ron," he said, "you need to go back to where your joy is." I remembered how Jesus had come to me as a little boy and met my needs. I heard clearly from the Holy Spirit, "Ron, if you stay where you are, you will die. But if you come back, I will give you life and I will give you life abundantly. You will be loved and cared for. Your greatest desire will be met."

God blessed my mother and I with a year of reconciliation before her death in 1988. From 1987 to 1990 the Lord dealt with me about my drugs and my alcohol, but not my homosexuality. On June 21, 1990, sitting alone in my living room, thumbing through God's Word, I opened it up to I Corinthians 6:11 "and such were some of you." No one ever told me I could be free from this. But, Jesus did! He came to me right there at home and through His Word said, "I can heal you, I can set you free."

My walk away from homosexuality was slow but progressive. During the first two years I cried so much, spread out on the floor, I thought grass would grow in my carpet.

But the tears washed my soul. Accepting God's freedom in my life helped me to make different choices. I got rid of almost everything that reminded me of a past sexual partner, place or event. If I could not bring myself to remove the item, I would put it away so I would not see it. Even clothes, music and friends changed.

During this time, the Lord showed me how badly His church needs education on how to minister to people with homosexual struggles. I went to the pastor of the church I had been attending to seek support. He responded, "Pray about it, forget about it and don't talk about it." He could not look beyond my faults to my underlying need. Shortly afterwards, my Bible study group, rejected me after inquiring about my past. In my feelings of rejection, hurt and anger about the lack of support, I choose to return to the lifestyle for a short season.

During this season of rebellion, God taught me a lot about His grace and my lack of obedience. I learned how to be proactive in my prayer life. Whenever I would get tired or sleepy during my devotions, I would get up and move around. Several times I decided the best place to have my devotions was in a closet. A real one! When trying to memorize scripture, I would imagine seeing it painted above my doorpost or windowsills. When ever unhealthy thoughts or pictures would come into my mind, the Holy Spirit would help me release them to Jesus. Sometimes dreams, trips, events, places or images would come to me like TV footage. I had to rebuke them in the name of Christ and give them to Him. He takes whatever we give!

The first man I met who believed that Jesus could free me from homosexuality was a Director of an Exodus Ministry. In an initial meeting with him, I angrily asked, "Can Jesus heal me from homosexuality?" When he responded "Yes". I asked, "How do you know?" His response, "because He has healed me", melted my anger into tears. One week later, I meet fifteen other men who were on the same journey and within a month, I met a large number of men and women at my first Exodus Conference seeking the same kind of freedom I was. This ministry was the olive branch I needed to stay faithful.

Within a year of my first Exodus Conference I applied and was accepted to Love in Action. The Lord showed me that I needed a safe place to walk through my relational issues. It was in the LIA program that I became very aware of my sinful nature.

For me, LIA redeemed group living, opened my eyes to see emotional entanglement as sin and helped me define healthy boundaries. God used my season at LIA to redeem my trust of others, especially care givers or authority figures. I became aware of how my actions had hurt others.

A struggle that I walked through at LIA centered around Romans 7:18, "I know hat I am rotten through and through as far as my old sinful nature is concerned..." I believed I deserved better than what God was saying. Out of pity and pride I lashed out at others exclaiming that life had been unfair that I was not rotten. Jesus, out of His love, showed me grace and mercy as I struggled with the holiness if God.

My life was in fact out of control. With thanksgiving I now realize, how my leaders at LIA committed to walk with me and with their hearts they helped me to learn to "sit in it" without running. God had a plan and Love In Action helped me to prepare for it.

The transformation in my life since 1990 has been unmistakable. Drugs, alcohol, pornography and homosexuality are no longer a part of my life.

At one time my thoughts were consumed with darkness. Now I wake up in the morning singing and now know because of the blood of Jesus I can take authority over my sin nature which used to so easily beset me.

He has redeemed the call he gave me at age fourteen to share the good news of redemption. I answered his call to minister to those who struggle with homosexuality and other sexual addictions in May 1996 by starting a ministry named Beyond Imagination in Raleigh, North Carolina.

"Drugs, alcohol, pornography and homosexuality are no longer a part of my life."

God has always given more than I could imagine. In 1996 He provided exceedingly abundantly above what I could ever think or imagine (Ephesians 3:20) by bringing me a very special woman. Ann Marie and I were married one year later on June 28. My story of his healing and redemptive power is still being lived out. I have tasted that the Lord, He is good!

"From Darkness to a Life Beyond Imagination" by Ron Elmore, Copyright ©1998, Used with permission.

(AP Photo/Charles Krupa, Copyright 2004, used with permission)

Gay couples line up outside Boston City Hall, waiting to apply for marriage licenses in Boston, Monday May 17, 2004.

19

All Things Became New

By

Donald L. Johnson

I was born in Mount Vernon, Westchester County, New York. I was raised on the south side of the city and grew up for the most part in the public housing projects. There are not many extraordinary things with regards to my being reared but I frequently recall those years with a mixture of grief and delight.

I was the fourth child born out-of-wedlock to my then 21-year old mother. My mother who migrated from a small coal mining town in West Virginia came to New York with the hope of finding employment, a better life and the fulfillment of her dreams. However, in her quest, she encountered several obstacles that led to her making some wrong choices. My conception and birth were the results of one of them.

I was conceived after she chose to succumb to a one night adulterous relationship. I knew little to nothing about my biological father for most of my life and I learned who he was in my late teens. It wasn't until I was 25 years old that I acquired enough to courage to introduce myself to him. All the while, he lived in the same community as I did.

My mother, early in her pregnancy decided to place me for adoption. As the adoption was prearranged, she never held or bonded with me. I was brought home from the hospital by my adoptive parents after my birth. The process was legalistic, prohibitive and somewhat strict.

I don't remember the first time being told I was adopted. My parents always apprised me of the situation but it was something that I was forbidden to discuss with anyone outside of the family. My being adopted was "a secret". Nonetheless it was something that I longed to talk about with anyone that would listen. Due much to my parents' inhibitions, the concealment became a source of insecurity for me. It helped to create an identity crisis and eventually led to confusion over my gender confusion. I acted much like a girl.

The mental disconcertion that I experienced as a child was often overwhelming. I was sometimes confused about my family dynamics and often perceived feelings of abandonment and rejection. One thing led to another. I began experimenting sexually with a god-brother who would visit our home when I was about 9 or 10 years old. I didn't know it but I opened the door for the spirit of homosexuality to enter into my spirit and life at that time. The Bible teaches that "the thief (Satan) comes not but for to steal, and to kill, and to destroy...." Saint John 10:10. It is worth mentioning that he, who introduced me to "same-sex" is in the penitentiary today for a drug related homicide.

My gender identity confusion became more evident by the time I was 12. By then, I was very effeminate and "girl like". Most of my friends were girls and I felt completely comfortable around them. I didn't identify much with masculine activities or care for sports and I felt often that I couldn't compete with boys my age. I was referred to psychological counseling due to the severity of the indications. School personnel finally concluded that it would be in my best interest to attend school on the opposite side of my town. The experience proved beneficial and it helped me stay focus and succeed academically. However, the main problem (of wanting to be a girl) had not been resolved. At the end of the school term my life took a drastic turn.

I was 14 years old when I completed junior high school and was experiencing adolescence, quite naturally. My mind set started to change and I began relinquishing many of the values and things that were dear. I became rebellious to my parents for the first time in my life and started keeping late hours, drinking alcohol and smoking marijuana. Something beyond what I was accustomed to began "driving me".

"My gender identity confusion became more evident by the time I was 12. By then, I was very effeminate and 'girl like.'"

That summer I found myself in the company of a group of male homosexuals. They were all older than me and immediately took me in. I felt like I had found my niche. I started convincing myself and eventually believed that I was supposed to be "gay and live that way. I came "out of the closet" so to speak and adopted the "gay lifestyle" when I was 14 years old. My life really changed.

Before long, I was frequenting "gay bars and nightclubs" and involved in many promiscuous activities with mostly older men. I started ingesting heroin on a regular basis, also. Eventually, I lost control.

I barely graduated from high school and tried to go on to college. However, I was "strung out" on heroin, had been twice arrested twice, served a brief sentence in jail and I was on probation. In college, things got worse.

I was using heroin when I would come for visits from school breaks and then I'd indulge in LSD, mescaline, hashish and marijuana when I was on the college campus. The homosexual activity continued while I was in college and I ended up contracting a severe case of a STD. I eventually returned to New York.

I was still in my early 20s and continued to be sexually involved illicitly and drug dependent. I tried to break the heroin dependency by enrolling in a methadone program and used prescription drugs: Valium, barbiturates and amphetamines to get high. This continued for about 15 years. Finally, after becoming an alcoholic, poly-substance abuser and a very active homosexual, I "lost it all." I experienced three (3) emotional/nervous breakdowns in 1987-88 and was hospitalized each time. The very event that I feared would happen, took place (Job 3:25). However, what the devil meant for evil, God intended it for my good. I had experienced several homosexual relationships but most of the them were of an abusive nature. My self-image and confidence were mostly shattered. I became to seek God for restoration by reading the scriptures. Also, while hospitalized for psychiatric reasons, I told the Lord that if he'd restore my mind and my spiritual health that I would serve him the rest of my life. The Lord heard my cry!

One day, in 1987 my biological mother Johnnie Lee Watson (who by then was saved and filled with the Holy Spirit) said to me, "Donald your problem is not psychiatric, it's spiritual". She had said that to me so many times but this time, the words rang in my ears. I said to her, "You mean to tell me that there is a spiritual solution to all that I've been experiencing for the last 21 years?" She responded by saying "Yes, and you need to be saved." Suddenly, it all made sense.

I decided resolutely that if my psychiatric and psychological dilemmas; drug and pill dependencies; deliverance from homosexuality and abuse against my own body could be accomplished through "getting saved" then salvation must be my answer. I decided to attend my mother's church, The Bible Church of Christ in Mount Vernon, New York.

It was April, 1987. I arrived at the church a short while after one of their deliverance services had begun. I had heard so much about the pastor, Bishop Roy Bryant, Senior who was conducting the service that day. I was told how God had taught Dr. Bryant everything that he knew and a part of his ministry was "casting out evil spirits" just as Christ had done. I had faith in bishop and I was impressed to see how he took time to teach the word of God to the people. Then, he would labor in prayer with them and dislodge unclean spirits. Hallelujah!

I didn't know what to expect, however, as the deliverance service, progressed it became evident that the power of God was present to heal, deliver and to set his people free. I decided to get on the prayer line, anxiously. The time came when Bishop Bryant reached me on the line and he stretched forth his hand and laid it upon my forehead. A miracle took place. I felt my feet lifting up from the ground and I heard myself speaking in an audible but unknown language. That was the day which the Lord had made. Though sinful I was, God through the baptism of the Holy Ghost ushered me into the mystical body of Christ. I was transformed.

The transformation of being a new creature in Christ Jesus has been a process. I began as a newborn baby and today 15 years later, I can truly say that I am free from homosexuality, insecurity, identity confusion and drug dependence. Old things are passed away and behold all things are become new (II Corinthians 5:17).

"Though sinful I was, God through the baptism of the Holy Ghost ushered me into the mystical body of Christ. I was transformed."

I am ordained minister of the gospel of Jesus Christ. And, now I go into all the world and preach the gospel to every creature. I volunteer as a chaplain at several correctional facilities throughout New York and work with youth as a county probation officer. I look forwarding to completing a MPA degree this summer and most of all I'm living for the Lord. Yes, Jesus saves. He also delivers, sets free and gives us the victory!

"All Things Became New" by Donald L. Johnson, Copyright © 2004, Used with permission.

(AP Photo/Josh Reynolds, Copyright 2004, used with permission)

Keith Maynard, 53, left, and Chip McLaughlin, 52, both of Cambridge, Mass., receive applause from the crowd as they walk down the front steps of City Hall in Cambridge, Mass., early Monday, May 17, 2004. They were among the first of several hundred same sex couples to apply for marriage license applications as Massachusetts became the first state in the U.S. to legalize same-sex unions.

20
Life After 911

By

Stephanie Boston

Giving Honor to God who has reclaimed His headship in my life. You see twelve days after 9-11 occurred, I received my own 9-1-1. While sitting on a bus I began to ask myself some questions about my life. If I leave this world today....How would I fare? Was God pleased with me ? Is it really alright for me to be both gay and Christian? I opened the Bible and began to read.. The words were so clear it was like reading them for the first time. My heart was convicted. I knew the truth. All I could do was cry and apologize over and over. I could hear a small voice say, " I don't want you to die that way, I want to save you , come back to me." That night I surrendered and gave Him control over my life again

Allow me to give you a little background at this point. You see I first accepted Christ on my own as a young girl at St. Luke's A.M.E. Church. I was in the choir, on the usher board, YPD, and the Rosebuds. I loved church. I loved the Lord.

Then at age 11 something changed. I had an uncle who offered my parents the opportunity to send me away to school for a better education. [How many of you know all opportunities aren't golden?] This sounded great to them. So at age 11 with bags packed I was off to school 150 miles away from home. Eleven years old I still needed the nurturing of my mother. I still needed the guidance and protection of my father. Eleven years old I still needed the family roots found in my grandmother. Eleven years old I still needed to interact with my brother and others of the male gender. Eleven years old I still needed my church and my God .

These were legitimate emotional needs. The question was for the next three years ; how was I going to meet them? You guessed it these young girls became everything I missed at home and more. Well the three years passed and I looked forward to going home....only to find out that they had found a high school just like the one I had finished. This one was 130 miles away from home. Three years now becomes seven. Fourteen years old I still had the same emotional needs and some new ones. Same environment , more girls.

Anyway, I graduated at the top of my class. Response....Oh this education really worked out for you. We're going to send you to college......Judson College for Women. Do you see a pattern here? Four more years and seven becomes eleven long years away from home. Away from a mothers love, away from a fathers guidance, away from a siblings sharing, away from the awareness of the male gender, away from my church and my God.

By now my reality is distorted. I am detached from my family and my church. God is somewhere in the distance. I returned home after finishing all this schooling to begin working. Somewhat disconnected from the family I once knew. They knew little about the private life I led all those years away from home. In a short time I was introduced to my mothers' new found religion; Jehovah's Witnesses. They were so strict and so disciplined that I thought surely this was a way for me to get back to God. For seven years it worked, I didn't touch another woman but I was miserable. I asked God for help. I asked the elders for help. Their answer was just pray and don't give in. I wondered how.

My questions were, "What about transformation?" and "doesn't Gods' word promise that a change would take place and a new creature would emerge?" Instead I was just repressing my feelings and feeling sick. Still the same pat answer, just pray and don't give in. Well I slipped one night and I felt relieved. [How many of you can relate?....Amen] Two more times and I felt good. [How many of you know I was crying out for help?] The elders had another talk with me and this time I was put out of the organization. I was no longer allowed to communicate with my mother. Yeah, you may wonder as I did where was Gods' grace, mercy, and His divine love in this action. [We need another support group for that one.]

"These were legitimate emotional needs. The question was for the next three years ; how was I going to meet them? You guessed it these young girls became everything I missed at home and more."

Needless to say I was crushed. I was deliberately rejected by the friends I had known for the past seven years. [Do you know what I did next?] I moved into a new circle of friends who loudly said God loves you just as you are. [Uuuuh!?] God knew you before you were born. God knew who you were going to love and it's okay. [WOW] Celebrate your difference it's a gift from God. I was free to be me. I embraced the lifestyle wholeheartedly. I went to a gay affirming church, sang in the choir, marched in the parades shouting; I'm gay and I'm proud! I was even a part of a temptation style all girl group. We didn't lip sync. No, we made up our own steps and wore the most debonair outfits. Oh we made the women whine when we performed. I was happy and life was good..

Then 9-11 happened and I was not sure if I died that I would see God. We are back to where we opened . My prayer on that bus ....." God be my Lord and my Savior again, I surrender all." I'm marching in a different parade now and I'm shouting ..."I'm saved and I'm proud."

Before 9-11 by invitation in February of 2000 I came to visit St. James. I liked the service and kept coming. But I still had the mindset that it was okay to be Christian and gay. For a whole year I still walked in that arrogance; coming to church with a suit and tie on. [Talk about a patient God] New Years' Eve of 2001 my relationship with God became very important. I read the Bible more, prayer picked up, attendance increased at St. James and decreased at the gay church. I inquired about a support group but there wasn't one to be found in this area. One day though I heard someone give their testimony on a Christian radio station of how they had been delivered from homosexuality. I wrote the station for information. They sent me the name of an international organization whose mission is to help persons who struggle with homosexuality. They still didn't have any groups in this area but they had an extensive book list. I found these books to be very helpful and they spoke specifically to my sin.[God is Good.] Just before the women's retreat a minister provided me a name and number of someone who had personally struggled and been delivered. She made herself available for prayer, for conversation or any questions I might have. [How many of you know that the devil wasn't happy] He tried to get busier than God. I lost money, bills started piling up, I lost my job, my apartment, my car and I was rushed to the hospital three times for anxiety attacks. As old friends, things, and activities were removed from my life loneliness set in and there was a big vacuum to be filled. [But God was still in control] At the women's retreat I ran into a minister who I grew up with at St. Luke's. We caught up on old times for lunch . As we were talking she recalled that there was a support group that met in Perth Amboy. [Nothing but God] I went to my first meeting in July 2002. The group was loving, in touch, and down to earth. The evidence of Gods' touch and orchestration made me want to dance around that room. The silence was broken. I was encouraged by others fighting the same fight. Supported by those who could relate. Hopeful that if God could do it for them, He could do it for me. God too wants you to grow spiritually, numerically, financially, and emotionally. [Luke 9:11]

21
Love Won Out

By

Mike Haley

Transcription of Mike Haley's testimony at the Focus on the Family Love Won Out Conference, Seattle, May 1999.

Good morning. Revelation 12:11 says "they overcame him by the power of the blood, the word of their testimonies, and they did not love their lives so much as to shrink back." Giving my testimony is not something that is my favorite thing to do but the most exciting part of it is that I see that God's word talks about us talking about how he helps us to come out of things in our life and I think that we – we owe that to individuals that are struggling through things. So I've made an attempt to, whenever I'm given the opportunity, to be able to profess what he's done in life and it's a very exciting thing to help somebody. But one of the things that I've done in my working with youth is I always try to make a stand to say, you know that the true testimonies of God's provision and God's grace are those people that don't get involved in things and come out of it. I really believe that those are the kids and the people that are the heroes, those that maintain their virginity and different things like that so I always like to state that, especially when I speak to a group of youth.

Let me get started with my own testimony. I was born in Southern California. I was raised and brought up in a family that had a very strong spiritual heritage. Years and years back my family has always been very involved in church and very excited about what the Lord has done in our family. I have two older sisters that are ten and twelve years older than myself, so when I was born, Dad was very excited that there was going to be a son. My dad owned sporting goods in Southern – sporting goods stores in Southern California so his desire for me was that I was going to be the best football player, best baseball player, best basketball player, best everything I could possibly be. But I chose to be a swimmer which was a sport that Dad thought was kind of a sissy sport, you know, and we've always kind of joked in our family because I could have had the best, you know, the latest Nike's of the best shoulder pads or the best Rider helmet, but you know, I chose a sport that took a piece of material about this big and a little pair of plastic goggles. So that's always kind of been a joke in our family.

But growing up as a kid, Dr. Nicolosi talks about the importance of the disidentification with the feminine and the identification with the masculine. That didn't happen for me in my life. What happened was, my dad, his way of making me a man was that he thought that he was going to push me in areas of sports that I wasn't interested in and then when I would get frustrated, he would do such things as call me Michelle, call me his third daughter, different instances like that. So times with my father became very painful. So the disidentification process with the feminine never occurred because times of being with my dad and being involved in masculinity were times of pain. So that never happened for me.

As I continued to grow up I realized that I really, really wanted my father's attention but I was much safer being in the area with my mom and my two older sisters. I remember one time when I was little, I was five and I had a pitch back. You know what those are? That's where – it's a little metal sheet thing and it's got a net in it and you throw a ball in it and the ball bounces back. You know, it's one of those toys for a kid that doesn't have any friends. I had one of those, and I remember Dad was teaching me how to bat and he said, you know, okay, now let's learn to switch hit. I'm five years old. I see the trampoline over in the corner. I have attention span of a five year old. Dad gets frustrated cause I'm not as interested in what he wants me to become. I'm wanting to run off to the trampoline. Dad would say, you know, why don't you just go in the house and be with your mom and your sisters, that's where you'd rather be anyway. I think he perceived it as a rejection.

"So the disidentification process with the feminine never occurred because times of being with my dad and being involved in masculinity were times of pain."

Now that I've talked to my dad about these things, we've seen a lot of what happened. There was a lot of my perception going on and a lot of his perception and him really not knowing how to deal with it. But I was starving for male affirmation and attention. I wanted nothing more than my dad to raise me in his arms and say, you know, you're the best son – the best thing that ever happened to me. I love you. And life would have been probably a little bit better. But that didn't occur. What happened for me was at the age of – at the age of eight though – as I said, we were raised in the church. All of us were raised in the church. And at the age of eight I accepted the Lord and I really do believe that for me that experience that happened to me at the age of eight was a very real experience. I knew Jesus as well as an eight year old can know Jesus and I wanted him in my heart and I do believe that was a very real thing. But I also began to feel some of what Dr. Nicolosi was saying was some of that difference. I began as I said to continue to grow up starving for my dad's affirmation and attention.

At the age of eleven there was a man that began to work for my father, began to pay this attention to me. It was unbelievable. He took me to the beach, taught me how to surf, took me to Disneyland, took me to the latest movies. It was just a wonderful relationship. I really felt like for once I found some worth when I was with this guy. He would affirm me for my body. You know, he always said, you know, you have a very lean body. Different things like that. And what I started to realize was this, I felt some kind of value or some kind of worth when I was with him. The problem was is that attention turned sexual so from the age of eleven to the age of eighteen I was a victim of sexual abuse. And I can say victim of sexual abuse today because I know that no twenty-seven, twenty-eight, twenty-nine year old should be sleeping with an eleven, twelve, and thirteen year old boy. But Proverbs 27:7 says the man that's full loathes honey but to him who is starving even what is bitter tastes sweet" and I was so starving for male affirmation and attention that when I had this bitter substitute I gobbled it up.

And I found on the way here this book. I was reading the Sacred Romance. And I've often tried to explain this to people and it's hard for people to understand but I found this in this book and it's an incredible statement. I'd just like to read it to you real – very quick. It says,

Very seldom are we ever invited to live out of our hearts. If we are wanted we are often wanted for what we can offer functionally. If rich, we are honored for our wealth; if beautiful, for our looks; if intelligent, for our brains. So we learn to offer only those parts of us that are approved, living out of a carefully crafted performance to gain acceptance from those who represent life to us.

And this man represented life. He represented male, masculine life for me. And this goes on further to say, "We divorce ourselves from our hearts and begin to live a double life." And that's exactly what happened for me. So this happening with the sexual abuse, my dad telling me at times that I'm feminine, in you know, more or less words, and then growing up on campuses, hearing the words fag and sissy and queer, that label went on very quickly. I felt different. I knew that this was the label that defined who I was. So in junior high it was a very tough time for me. I wanted to fit in. My family never knew about the sexual abuse until later but I remember as a young boy, eleven, twelve, and thirteen, at school I would be throwing up constantly. I would be in a class – I had permission in all of my classes to leave any time I wanted because I would just throw up. My parents thought I had an ulcer. They thought it was because I was swimming and swimming was becoming intense. I was at this point holding age group records in Orange County. So I was very good at what I was doing there but didn't get Dad's affirmation because it wasn't a sport that he was interested in.

High school was very difficult again for me. I grew up and what worked for me in the gay life – and by now I'm sixteen years old. I can drive and I'm not far from Laguna Beech and for those of you that don't know Laguna Beech, Laguna Beech is equivalent to probably San Francisco in Southern California. So very quickly I learned where I could go to receive this type of affirmation and approval and I used what I had. I was a blond, young surfer boy and that's a very prime commodity in Southern California. So I was very approved and very much embraced into homosexuality. I went to the gay beaches, went to the gay bars. And you say, how does a sixteen, seventeen, eighteen-year-old boy get into gay bars? It's very easy in certain societies to be able to do that.

"…I was so starving for male affirmation and attention that when I had this bitter substitute I gobbled it up."

So I totally embraced my homosexuality, continued to grow up and really had this whole thing going on where I loved the Lord on this hand with all of my heart and stayed involved in church this entire time I was growing up. I was the kid that was always there when the doors were open. But on the weekends as well I was also at the gay bars, at the gay beech, at the gay gym, seeking that approval and that worth. It was really the only time I felt the worth because when I was in church, what I heard was that homosexuality is an abomination. And yes, God's word says that and I believe that with all my heart. One thing Southern Baptists do right is teach God's in-errant word. And that is later the thing that helped me walk out. But I would hear homosexuality is an abomination and how that would work for me is homosexuality is an abomination. I'm a homosexual. Therefore, I'm an abomination. So church became a very uncomfortable place for me to be. It wasn't – I wasn't hearing about – I was hearing about the power of Jesus but I wasn't hearing about the power of Jesus to save homosexuals. So I just thought we were the scum of the Earth so church didn't become a place that I wanted to go.

The gay community was waiting with open arms and man, it was there, it was the approval, it was the worth that I needed as a young boy. I continued to grow up and did a lot of things. I would go to the Christian camps. I remember one summer being at Hume Lake. I was fifteen and I said, "Lord, you've got to take this thing away from me. I want to serve you. I want to know you with all that I am. I'm not going to stop praying until you take this gay thing or whatever is going on in my life away." I remember kneeling next to my bed and just praying, "Lord, I'm not going to stop praying" – you know, only to fall asleep and wake up feeling just as gay, just as different as I had when I started to pray. Remember going to Hume Lake when I was fifteen and I really felt this call in my life to want to rededicate my life. I always really wanted to serve the Lord and just continue to try to do things and do things.

The performance that this book talked about I performed and performed, thinking that if I was just good enough, God would take it away. And I went forward and I really felt like the Lord called me into full time Christian service in the area of youth. So I really had tthat on my heart and the memory is emblazoned in my mind. As I continued to grow up I got more and more involved in homosexuality. It just continued to suck me in. I found more and more worth within that lifestyle. I went again and was struggling – I'm into my twenties now and I bought into the lies that I was being taught, that I was hearing. When I was in high school, I did go for counseling at one point and said, this is what I'm feeling. The counselor said to me, you know, you're born this way, you just need to accept that this is how God has made you. So when you're a struggling adolescent and you go to someone that you trust and this is what you hear, these things become reality, they become your reality. They become the thing that you hold onto. So as much as I didn't want to hold onto that, I had to because it's what I knew and what I was starting to trust. It became very – I became very depressed. There was no way out.

Dr. Nicolosi talked about the suicide rate and I believe personally that yes, gay kids are at risk but I think it's because we're telling them that there is no hope rather than a homophobic society. So I continued to grow up. I went to Biola University. Again, as you can see, continued the Christian thing. For those of you that don't know, Biola is a Christian college down in Southern California, Bible Institute of Los Angeles. I did really well there. I wanted, again, like I said, my degree was in Christian education, you know, was helping in the church with the youth, but again, involved in the bars on Friday and Saturday night. It was just an incredibly miserable time in my life, this double life that I was living. But I didn't, I wasn't hearing any way to get help. Like I said, I was at Biola and I'm in my twenties now and was very much still continuing the struggle and wanting to believe that there was a way out.

One day I was at a gay gym and I was – found myself in an illicit situation with another individual. We got outside the gym and he said to me, he said, I'm sorry, I can't go on any further with this, and I'm trying to walk away from homosexuality. That was the first time that I had heard about that, was in an illicit situation with another gay man that was struggling to walk away from it. And I thought, you know, what are you talking about – you're born gay. I began to, you know, all the rhetoric, I just began to spew on this guy cause I had bought into it. So he said, well, let's get in my car and I want to drive around and talk to you about this because for two gay men, or two men to be in a car in front of this gym was not a good thing. Not like I cared or anything, but I just thought, okay, you know, we'll get in this car and drive around. So we began to drive around and he was talking about his friend named Jeff Conrad and he said, this man is studying the root causes of homosexuality and how a person can walk away from this and what a person needs in their life to walk away from this life dominating characteristic and I just was listening to it buy yet I was hesitant. Mind you, this is 11:45 at night. The gym closes at midnight. It's 11:45 at night. We're driving around Mission Viejo, California and he says, let's pull into this parking lot over here and talk about it. So we pulled into another parking lot – he began, he was continuing to tell me about this man named Jeff Conrad. All of a sudden his eyes got really big and he goes, oh, my gosh, there he is right now. I got the goose bumps and I felt the Lord say to me, was my arm too short

"As I continued to grow up I got more and more involved in homosexuality. It just continued to suck me in."

to rescue you? And I just knew it was my turn to shut up and the Lord had something for me. So he motioned Jeff over to the car. To make a long story short, Jeff had taken one shift, he worked at Ruby's on the pier in Balboa Island and had taken one shift that night at the Mission Viejo Rubies, had never worked there before, but you know, you can see the coincidence of it all. But anyway, Jeff came over to the car and I was leaving in two weeks to go work at Hume Lake again, as a counselor this time, not as a student. Again, serving the Lord to see if my homosexuality would kind of take care of itself. But he said, well, what I'll do is I'll write you while you're gone.

And this began a 5 to 7-year process were Jeff would write me back and forth. I would move. I did a lot of different things. Like I said, went away to school. In this book, You Don't Have to be Gay is the culmination of that relationship. This is probably – well, this is the best book for teen boys that are struggling with homosexuality because what it shows is the positive male relationship – positive non-sexual male relationship and also discusses how to walk away from homosexuality and what some of the root causes are and it's really encouraging to be able to read this because for a kid, you feel like you're in somebody's mail because it's written in letter form, like it might say, April 1st, you know, dear Mike, blah, blah, blah, and it shows the relationship, so kids really like to read it because it's fun. It's not just a basic boring kind of psychological book. So I highly recommend that and that is on sale at the bookstore. So anyway, continued like I said to delve into homosexuality cause I didn't trust this. I didn't trust these things that Jeff was telling me.

So what does any good boy do when he graduates from Christian undergraduate? He goes off to seminary. So I applied for seminary in Southwestern Baptist Theological Seminary, got accepted, walked through the doors of that seminary and began thinking, now I'm away, I've moved again. What you'll notice a lot of times with the gay men is they do a lot of times where they move, especially those of us that are trying to get out of it. You know, it's the relocation idea. If I get somewhere else it'll take care of itself. But you know when you move somewhere you take your luggage with you everywhere you go and my luggage was there with me. So it wasn't very long until I discovered Dallas and went there and finally I just got sick and tired of being sick and tired with this whole double life. I left seminary after a semester and I just said forget it. I came out to my family. I came out at work and it was just this freedom that I felt. I met the perfect guy in Dallas and I just thought this is it. I can be the one gay Christian that does this and can do it right.

But yet I knew because I was still frustrated with seminary that it was going to take a lot to make that happen. He and I would go to church together at Prestonwood Baptist in Dallas and it just became again a life of just miserable things. He was – like I said – the perfect male. I thought, oh, okay, if I come out to my family and they see and aren't homophobic and start to see and embrace me and him and our relationship, then, then my life will be better. That didn't help. If we – then I thought, oh, we just need to buy a home. If we can buy a home and settle down and I can have the security of a home, then that will help. That didn't help. Well, what about looking into adopting? I've always wanted kids. I knew that I was not going to be able to have kids – that I was – you know, I'd flushed that years ago because I was gay and gays, you know, can't have kids unless they adopt or artificially inseminate. And we were looking towards doing that. All these things I kept doing and doing, thinking that it would make me happy and I just continued to get more and more miserable. My family this whole time was very open, still very open, but I knew their stance on homosexuality. They didn't talk to me all the time. They didn't say, you know this is wrong, you know this is wrong. Instead what they did is they opened their home. I would go home for Thanksgiving, would take my lover with me at the time.

By the way, this was a two-year relationship which was for me, I considered that my long-term relationship involved in homosexuality and we were both, it was open on both ends of our relationship so the whole monogamous thing as Dr. Nicolosi talked about is just an absolute fallacy. But I would continue to go home and I found love and acceptance in my home. My sisters were going on in their lives. They were getting married. They were having kids. I would go home for Thanksgiving and I would think, you know, this is really what I want. This is really what I want. I would grab my nieces and nephews. I would hold them. And you know, I'd be watching. Sorry. And I would just, I would just weep to myself. You know, my family would see it every once in a while. But, they're like what's wrong. And I'd say, you know, I just miss watching the kids grow up. And that wasn't the reality. The reality was I thought, I can never have this. You know, I've ruined my life. I can never have this.

"All these things I kept doing and doing, thinking that it would make me happy and I just continued to get more and more miserable."

So I went on and I finally had reached my end and become so miserable in Dallas, I called Jeff and I called my family and I said, look, I've had enough of homosexuality. My life is more than being a homosexual man. I went to gay hairdressers, gay beach, gay gym, everything I did was homosexuality. I thought, there's got to be more to life than homosexuality. And Budd – I mean Budd – Jeff, that's my nickname for him. Jeff would continue to write me over the years and finally I just said, if the Jesus that Jeff Conrad knows, if he can be that faithful to me, surely the Jesus that Jeff Conrad knows can be that much more faithful to me so I wanted to get to know the Jesus that Jeff represented to me. It wasn't the Jesus that I'd heard about this distant Jesus in church but it was a Jesus that loved me and died for me even in the midst of my homosexuality. So I called and I said, I want to come home. My brother-in-law said, Mike, there's only one place for you. That's in our home. Come home.

That was in the year, I left lifestyle in December of 1989, came home and I failed miserably in 1990. I was actually counseling with Joe Dallas, not that that's any representation of his counseling by any means. I was just – I was a mess. I was a sexual addict. I was absolutely a sexual addict. To let you know how deep I got into homosexuality, a couple years earlier I had been arrested for prostitution. The ultimate was if a man was willing to pay for me, if he would expend that commodity on me, I knew that that somehow gave me worth. So anyway, came home, and that summer Jeff said to me, there's this conference called Exodus. I think we need to go. So I said, okay. I want to do whatever I can. I went there. Make a long story short, I heard about a residential program through Exodus that was housed in San Raphael, California. I thought, this is what I need. Because two years later, the previous two years I had been working in adolescent treatment with kids that were in long term treatment so I saw the ability that kids were able to have walking out of whatever they were involved in through people being around them twenty-four hours a day and I thought, you know, I'm a sexual addict. This is what I need.

So I went to this program and I thrived. I did incredibly well. It says our boundaries are set in pleasant places and that's exactly what they did for me. They said, Mike, this is the left side of the road. There's run away cars over here and if you go over there you're going to get damaged. Here's the right side of the road. There's thorn bushes and everything else over here. If you run between these two lines, you can run. And man, I took that and I did. I ran. I did incredibly well. I just thought, this is what I'm looking for. I'm looking for people to slap me upside the head when I need that and I'm looking for people to provide the loving shoulder when I needed that. And that's what that program provided. I applied for my teaching credential while I was there because again, I remembered this call on my life to want to work with youth but yet I knew that I couldn't be a youth pastor which I had originally started to do because I used to be gay and that just wasn't going to happen. So I applied for my teaching credential and was refused because I had a sexual arrest on my record. So I became very angry at God. I thought, you know, you've called me into wanting to work with youth and now this is what's happening.

So like I said, I continued to do very well and I just thought, well, maybe this is what I'm supposed to do is work for Love and Action. So I went through the ranks and I finally got on staff with Love and Action, not to mention that when I got back home that summer in 1990, from Exodus, I met a girl named Angie and she was dating my best friend. They broke up and we became very close friends and she was a woman that began to walk beside me in this whole process. So to make a long story short, I worked for Love and Action and they decided that they were going to relocate to Memphis, Tennessee, so I moved with them. Within this time I had gotten engaged. I got married December 4th, '94 at four o'clock. It's a easy one to remember and helps me stay out of trouble. So anyway, we got married, went on a week's honeymoon to Cancun and moved cross country to Memphis, Tennessee.

You take two Southern Californians, move them to Memphis, Tennessee and ah, it was not a pretty sight. But anyway, we were there. We showed up. I just have to tell you this real quickly. We showed up. We had no warm clothes. We wore shorts. We were tanned. It was the middle of December. People were looking at us like we were crazy. We were. But anyway, we got there and I began to become very disillusioned in my position with Love and Action. I thought, you know, I really want to be reaching youth.

I thought, there's got to be more to life than homosexuality.

Well, my pastor's 30th anniversary was that year of time that he had been at the church. A man came and spoke at our church and I just absolutely blanked out on his name – Tony Campolo. Tony Campolo came and spoke at our church that day and alls I remember him talking about was how God's call is irrevocable and that went so deep into my heart because you know what I would do in my life is I would say, God's grace is sufficient except for me because I was a homosexual. God's grace is sufficient except for me because I was arrested for prostitution. I always had these conditions on it but what I had to realize is that God's grace is sufficient, period. And what happens so many times in our life is that we minimize because of our own guilt and our own anguish and I just think Jesus is up there saying, "Look what I did for you on the cross. I died for you and you're slapping me in the face by not owning what I have for you." So I continued to hear this and really wrestle through this whole issue. So two weeks later after Tony was there, the youth position had opened up at the church to be a youth pastor, so I thought, you know, alls they can say is no. I'm sure they will. It's the buckle of the Bible belt. I used to be gay, was arrested for prostitution. It's working with their kids and you know, of course, they're going to say no.

Nine months later, nine months later I went through a very long application process, gave my testimony to the parents, gave my testimony to the kids, talked to all the elders. I mean, it was like, hello? Let me hear what you guys have to say about your lives. You know, let's get real here. Anyway, nine months later they gave me the position and it was a dream come true. It was unbelievable. The Lord restored me to the point where I could be a youth pastor at a church in the South. It was unbelievable. So my wife and I thrived. What did I say that was funny, the whole South thing? So my wife and I thrived in this position. We were loving it. We were just incredible. It was an incredible time in our lives. The Lord was blessing us and I finally found my niche. It was – I was incredibly happy. I was away from the whole ex-gay movement, feeling a very normal life. And that was something that was just – I always wanted my whole life.

Well, last May I got a phone call. "Hello, this is John Paulk." I knew John. John was my house leader when I went through that residential program. "We have a position here at Focus and I feel like you're the one that's supposed to take it."

And I thought, "No thank you. I don't want to go back. I don't want to work for Focus, those right wing fundamentals, you know, I don't want to work there."

You know, that was my attitude. I'm away from the whole homosexual ministry. I have a normal life. I don't want it. I struggled intensely with that process. To make a long story short one night I was up struggling through this process, and like I said, I didn't want this. I didn't want to go back. The church doesn't really respect this ministry. The world, of course, talks about it in a negative light. And I was struggling with this and this is what I read:

"One night I got up and said, Lord, I just really need to hear from you. This is the will of God for me. I did not choose it. I sought to escape it. But it has come. Something else has come too: a sense of certainty that God does not want me only for a pastor. He wants me also for a leader. I feel a commissioning to work under God for the revival of this branch of his church. Careless of my own reputation, indifferent to the comments of older and jealous men. I am 36."

Guess how old I am?

"If I am to serve God in this way, I am no longer to shrink from the task but do it. I have examined my heart for ambition. I am certain it is not there. I hate the criticism I shall evoke and the painful chatter of people. Obscurity and the service of the simple people, my students, is my taste. But by the will of God this is my task. God help me. Bewildered and unbelieving I heard the voice of God say to me, I want to sound the note through you. Oh, God, did ever an apostle shrink from the task more? I dare not say no, but like Jonah I would feign run away."

And I read that and I thought. Okay, Lord, you couldn't be any more clear. So I sent my resume, got the position, and I'm now working at Focus. It's just been an absolute, incredible thing, to know that the Lord has brought me full circle, that he allowed me the dream of being a youth pastor so that now when I go and speak to youth pastors and they're saying, well, how can you talk to us, I can say, look, I was there with those kids. I know it works. I know how you can talk about homosexuality with those kids, how they can cling to it. And it's just been an incredible time.

"...whatever's happened in your life, God can pull you out of it."

Let me just share one last thing with you. About three weeks ago, my wife said, honey let's – we just moved into a new house. She said, honey, let's just go to bed early tonight. I'm tired, I don't want to move in. So I said, okay, that sounds great. She said, I have something I want to read to you. So she pulled out her Bible. She had to wake me up first. She pulled out her Bible and she read this to me and it says. *"Behold, children are a heritage from the Lord, the fruit of the womb is a reward. Like an arrow in the hand of a warrior, so are children in one's youth. Happy is the man whose quiver is full of them."* She said, "I have something for you." She pulled a quiver out of a box and she said, honey, here's your first arrow. We're pregnant. So after four years of trying, a lot of infertility tests, I'm a daddy. So, come December, I'm going to be a full fledged daddy and get to hold that thing for the first time.

But this is a message I just want to share with you guys, that whatever's happened in your life, God can pull you out of it. God has that dream that you've had and wanted. He's placed that in your heart and in your mind. So what I'm here today is to say to you, don't let your guilt and your remorse and the things that have happened to you stop you from what God has for you. Instead, embrace them and go on and see how He might turn around and use them for His good.

"Love Won Out" by Mike Haley, Copyright © 1999, Used with permission.

(AP Photo/Steve Miller)
Gay marriage supporters rally outside the State Capitol in
Hartford, Conn., Sunday, May 16, 2004.

22

Choosing God

By

Kevin D. Giles

For years I wanted to get rid of my homosexual attractions, behavior and lifestyle. You know how it is. I had a love-hate relationship with all things gay. I enjoyed the "freedom" homosexuality gave me – although I was bound by hiding. What a dichotomy! Some say that true freedom comes from "coming out of the closet". I believe that is where the real bondage begins.

When I first met "Dave", like all of the others, I thought he was the one. Except for the fact that we had sex on our second date… we took things "slow". *Go figure.* We thought we had the perfect relationship. We met at a Christian ministry. At the time, both of us were in pursuit of walking away from homosexuality. As we exchanged glances and smiles, we knew something was happening. Could it be? Could I actually have a intimate relationship with a *Christian* man? Could God actually bless this? In my mind, I knew better. I knew what the Word of God teaches on homosexuality. But my *wounded heart* had a different response.

Days became months as Dave and I built our relationship. Our lives became totally intertwined as we shut out other people and other interests. The longer we stayed together, the more like *him* I was becoming. I was slowly losing myself through a relationship – **again**. Although we prayed together, it was difficult incorporating my gay life with my Christian beliefs. After being together for a year, this struggle came to a head one Saturday morning. Dave called me stating that we needed to talk about the "problems" in our relationship. When he arrived at my apartment, he knocked on the door instead of using his key and stood outside. I opened the door and all he had for me was a challenge. He said, "**Choose me or choose God!**" I was shocked. I had been deceived into believing we both *were* choosing God. I was at a crossroad. I told him, "I'll choose you". I just didn't feel like I could let him go. Not yet. The next words out of his mouth surprised him more than me. He said, "No, you must choose the Lord." and he turned to walk away. In mid-stride, he turned back towards me and asked, "What did I just say?" As I stood there with my mouth hanging open, I knew the Lord had spoken through him. It was my "burning bush" experience. I knew I had to leave him and leave homosexuality. And that is exactly what I did. God put me on a new journey to discover the true me, to heal the hurts that lied to me, and break the chains that bound me. Homosexuality was and is a poor attempt to detach from the world of masculinity that you hate and has hurt you; a poor relationship with your father or the abuse from an older male. Homosexual activity is worse, an attempt to re-connect to men by having sex with them. It is an act of self-worship and idolatry that never truly satisfies.

Over the years, God has truly performed a marvelous work in my life. I am ever grateful to Him for restoring my manhood and my masculine and heterosexual identity. He has restored me enough to become a healthy and satisfied husband of 8 years, as well as a father of 3 and a foster father of 5. God has grown me from hating myself and hating being male to loving my maleness. I've learned to seek out and embrace the masculine within me. I am a man! I am God's man and I love it! I will never be the same. God has lead me to educate others on the transforming power of Christ and His cross. I do so through seminars, training and through my book, **Gay, But Not Happy**: *Dealing With Your Unwanted Homosexuality* (Released 2002).

"I knew what the Word of God teaches on homosexuality. But my *wounded heart* had a different response."

My encouragement for any gay man or struggling Christian who reads my book or this testimony is this: Yes, God definitely loves you… so much so that He would never want to leave you with the "band-aid" of homosexuality to inadequately cover the gaping wound in your gender identity. In Him, you can be healed from your hurts and restored to the awesome person God created you to be.

"Gay But Not Happy" by Kevin D. Giles, Copyright © 2003, Used with permission.

David Rudeurick, 34, center, and Michael Hight, 39, both of Somerville, Mass., kiss inside City Hall in Cambridge, Mass., on Sunday, May 16, 2004. The two were among the same sex couples who gathered to wait for marriage licenses to be issued at midnight, and marry later the same day, the first day on which Same Sex marriage became legal in Massachusetts on May 17, 2004.

23

My Journey Out of "the Life"

By

Steve Rooks

I experienced no childhood molestation or early affinity to the gay lifestyle. With the exception of having an emotionally distant father and being constantly teased and ridiculed by many of my peers, I had a "normal" childhood. It was not until I was in college that I had my first homosexual experience.

My partner was not the classic gay man. He was a star college athlete and by most observations a "lady's man." He was everything I felt I was not – secure in himself, strong and powerful but he was also willing to accept me for who I was.

Though I knew there was something inherently wrong about our first encounter, I was powerless to resist his advances. Although I also dated women at that time, he and I were sexually involved for almost all my college years.

It was not until my senior year in college that I began pondering the big issues of life. I spent a year and a half reading the Bible, hoping to discover who God is and who I was created to be. This pursuit continued after graduation.

"In February of 1983, I began my journey 'out of the life.'"

During my first year as a dancer in New York, I became involved in a number of relationships, the final one lasting for more than four years. I had somehow become convinced that God had made me gay and I would probably be that way for the rest of my life.

However, after I surrendered my life to Jesus Christ at the Brooklyn Tabernacle in 1981, I began to question my sexuality. In February of 1983, I began to question my sexuality. In February of 1983, I began my journey "out of the life."

I became one of the founding members of L.I.F.E. Ministry that year and was a counselor and leader in the ministry for a decade. Today, I am the leader of one of the ministry chapters.

I have been married for almost 15 years. I am a choreographer and instructor of dance, with my lovely wife, Desiree, and two daughters. I am thrilled to say I have been out of homosexuality for more than 21 years.

"My Journey Out of 'the Life" by Steve Rooks, Copyright © 2004, Used with permission.

24
My Struggle With Lesbianism

By

Bummi Niyonu Anderson

My struggle with lesbianism began when I was around 4 years old. I was too young to know I was gay; but I knew I was different. I knew I was drawn to a female cousin of mine. It was the beginning of my struggle for sexual identity.

My struggle manifested itself early in how I dressed (shorts, jeans and sneakers), how I behaved (playing sports and being a tomboy), and eventually how I chose my relationships. Somehow I developed a strong attraction for women, which led me into sexual and emotional relationships. I always ended up hurt, angry and deeply depressed. Sometimes I wanted to kill myself.

"Freedom in Christ has taught me that I can have healthy God-given relationships."

I got saved in 1997. At that time I was involved in a sexual relationship that I was enjoying. I did not come to Jesus because I was running from something or unhappy. I simply found a "greater love." I came out of the gay lifestyle when I realized God had greater plans and purposes for me.

The biggest thing salvation did for me was give me the freedom to choose. When I was in darkness, I saw myself as a lesbian and thought the only relationship I could ever have was a sexual relationship with a woman. Freedom in Christ has taught me that I can have healthy God-given relationships.

I learned that there is a process of deliverance from homosexuality, but salvation is the first step. Making the decision to follow Christ and repenting is essential.

The key to my freedom involved three things; seeking God in prayer, reading the Bible and developing healthy relationships. God spoke to me in prayer and through His Word, and He put people in my life who reinforced what God had already said about me.

"My Struggle With Lesbianism" by Bummi Niyonu Anderson, Copyright ©️ 2004, Used with permission.

25
Total Deliverance
By
Vanessa Jaudon

Since the age of six years old I have always had a sense of who God was. I can remember sitting and watching televangelist Jimmy Swaggart ministering and asking if anyone wanted to receive Jesus Christ as their personal Lord and Savior. I stood there that day with my grandmother and I lifted my hands up to Jesus, closed my eyes and asked the Lord to forgive me of my sins and come into my heart to live. From that day on when I went to church I would clap and sing with the choir. I even tried with all that was in me to understand what the preacher was saying. I would come home from church and instead of playing house I would play church with my cousins. I would pretend to be the choir director and I would pretend to be the preacher. During the summer we would go outside and sing the songs we learned at church the previous Sunday, and people would actually stand there and listen to us sing. I may have been young, but even then I knew that there was something that was different about me.

I left Philadelphia with my mother and brother and moved back to Tennessee with my father when I was in the second grade. These next few years were the start to some of the most painful years of my life. I recall every weekend my father would go to work on Saturday and come home with a pint of Vodka. By the time he woke up from his nap he would find something to argue about. It was so hard for me to understand why God would allow me to live the life I lived. Everyone walked on eggshells. My mother was a saved woman that truly loved the Lord, at the same time she was so submissive. I hated the fact that she would let my father talk to her in any way he wanted to. I felt like she wanted to take up for me when my father would have his episodes, but she didn't know exactly what to say. My older brother was blind and mentally challenged so there was nothing he could do. I felt so all alone, I can recall the pain I felt every Saturday. I would always try to find ways to go do something on the weekends. My father was always the providing type, but he was never the uplifting or affectionate one. He was physically abused as a child, but to him that was how it was supposed to be. It was then that I really started looking for love in all the wrong places.

When I was in third grade I recall a friend of my parents named Marie spent the night. She had been drinking and wanted to go up to my room to rest. I always respected Marie; she was one of the funniest women that I knew of. On that particular night Marie was talking about how much she missed her daughter that was killed by a drunk driver. After listening to her talk I recall waking up and she had her hand in my underwear and was touching me. I just laid there, and then a few minutes later she got up and went out the room. I didn't realize what was going on, but it was affection and for me I liked it. It was later when I met my friends Lisa, and

Sara that we were playing house and we would touch each other and do the things that we saw grown people doing as well as people on Lisa's older brother's porn movie do. I knew what I was doing was very wrong, but to me it was fun. It was always our little secret. I used to do this with all of my female friends that would come spend the night at my house. Each time we would teach each other different things. It got to the point where not only was it just female on female, it became threesomes. Then, on Sunday mornings we would go to church with my mom with no one every knowing that this was going on. To me this was not a lifestyle just some attention that my soul desired, but just couldn't get elsewhere.

"I recall waking up and she had her hand in my underwear and was touching me."

We moved to St. Louis, MO, where I went to high school. By the time I entered middle school I had already experienced my first incidents with pornography, masturbation, same sex encounters, and attempting to commit suicide. Most of these things had went on without anyone every finding out. When, I moved to St. Louis, I was determined that things had to change. The end of my seventh grade year I had my first serious relationships with a male. Allen gave me all of the attention and "love" that my father never gave me. My father was still drinking and situations seemed to get worse, so being with Allen was joy to my heart. It wasn't until a few months after being together Allen started to become verbally abusive. I couldn't believe it; once again I felt the same way I had felt with my father. My heart was shattered by a man. Allen hit me twice, but both times I defended myself. He apologized for hurting me, but within a few weeks he went back to his normal self. A few months before I turned fourteen Allen decided that he wanted to have sex. I was so scared, but if I wanted to keep this thing that I called love in my life I had to do what he said do. I hated having sex with Allen, I felt horrible.

Eventually, my relationship went downhill and I recall him telling me that he didn't want to be with me anymore. I was hurt because this was another male to let me down, but at the same time I was relieved to be free from him. That next Sunday I went to a new church Greater Grace with my mother. It was that Sunday that Pastor Larry Jones was ministering and he mentioned something about God wanting to fill that void in our lives with His Love. I cried and cried because that is what I had been waiting all my life to hear. It was that Sunday ---March 25-- that I gave my life to the Lord. For several months I was on fire for the Lord. For the first time, I had real, consistent relationship with God. He taught me how to pray and fast and enjoy just being in His presence. My mother and I would pray and talk about the Lord all of the time. I went to high school and would witness to everyone that I could. Then, all of a sudden my life took a turn. I met someone from my past and began to fornicate once again. I hated myself for turning on the Lord. Has this happened to you? If it has, please keep reading.

The one person that loved me the most without me having to do anything but receive it and share His love with others, I had let down. It was then, that Kristy begin spending nights with me. I knew when I first met her that there was something about her. She was a very touchy young lady. One night after going out to dinner she came back to my house and it was then after all of the years that passed that we fell into sexual temptations with one another. That happened several times and then once again with another female friend of mine. I could not believe what was going on. The madness was killing me! In the middle of me going crazy I recall a prophet telling me that the Lord was going to use me in a mighty way. The Lord spoke to me one day while I was in church and told me that He was going to use me in ministry. I knew that it was the Lord because right after He told me I asked Him to confirm it, and He did exactly what I asked. The problem that I had wasn't hearing God it was being obedient. It seemed like the more I wanted to be out of a life of having sex with males and females the more it kept coming up. The Lord spoke to me one day and said if you want be free then you have to get out of the environment that you are in and come after me! That next week I went on a seven day fast.

I believed with my whole heart that God would do it for me if I did what I was supposed to do. During that fast I went to a conference at my church New Birth Cathedral. It was there during an afternoon session I felt the chains break. I cried like I had never cried before and released all of the hurts and pains of rejection that lead me to believe that I had to have a man or a woman to fill in the void that was there. The Love of the Lord filled my life like never before. Bishop Long preached about knowing who we are in Christ. I asked God to tell me who I was in Him so that I could be the woman that He wanted me to be.

The next few years from then would be the foundation years of my new life. I was in college in Atlanta, Georgia, and in the Atlanta University Center you would see all kinds of things going on. I asked God, "why did you send me here?" His answer was so that I might be an example of His goodness. I went through so much hell all of my life but now I know my hell is the help that someone needed for their healing. I met people and began sharing my story of deliverance from a lifestyle of perversion. The Lord allowed me to walk with males and females that wanted to be set free from a lifestyle of homosexuality. I even entered into a relationship that I know at the time was God ordained with a male that dealt with homosexuality.

The most important thing for young people like me to understand about overcoming homosexuality is to be truthful so that God can use us to set someone else free. I believe that the Body of Christ is in bondage because many people are caught up in pride and fear and do not want to speak out about what the Lord has done in their lives.

" I cried like I had never cried before and released all of the hurts and pains of rejection…"

It was hard for me too, but during that time the Lord taught me how to pray for others that were struggling with that. He allowed me to have compassion towards them. My problem in the church was that no one would ever talk about my issues. I always heard the preachers talk about drinking and gambling. When they did talk about homosexuality they were saying that they were going to hell, so when I was doing my thing I felt like I couldn't go to anyone. When the Lord set me free I always wanted to allow people to know that, yes, the sin is wrong and God hates it, but He loves you so much that He is willing to do whatever needs to be done to get you free. Now, I live a life of total deliverance. I am not ashamed of who I was because it has molded me and made me who I am now in Christ. I just recently told my mother of my past and even started to have a good relationship with my father. I bless God for all that He is and all that He has done in my life and in the lives of others. I stand on this verse Matthew 6:33 in all that I do, *Seek ye first the Kingdom of God, and all His righteousness, and all these things shall be added unto you.* If God is able to do all of that for me I know without a shadow of a doubt He is able to do it for anyone!

"Total Deliverance" by Vanessa Jaudon, Copyright © 2004, Used with permission.

1/25/04 - Pro-Gay Marriage demonstration outside Cathedral High School, where the Mass. Voices for Traditional Marriage rally supporting traditional marriage is taking place inside in the school's auditorium.

26

The Days of Lot

By

Talbert W. Swan, II

The greatest event that the world has ever known will soon take place. Christians refer to this event as the rapture. It is the time referred to in scripture when Jesus will remove those that are saved from the earth in accordance with 1 Thessalonians chapter 4. This historic event will usher in a time of tribulation and turmoil. During this period, known as the "Great Tribulation," the anti-Christ will rise to power.

In Matthew 24:37, Jesus gave us a time-table for these events. He said, "But as the days of Noe were, so shall also the coming of the Son of man be." This brings up an obvious question: What were the days of Noah like? The Bible says in Genesis 6:11, "The earth also was corrupt before God, and the earth was filled with VIOLENCE." This is a perfect description of this current generation. Violence is commonplace and is a mainstay in the daily news across the country.

Another description of when the last days will come is found in Luke chapter 17: "Likewise also as it was in the days of Lot; . . . Even thus shall it be in the day when the Son of man is revealed." The days of Lot were characterized by Sodom and Gomorrah – acts of homosexuality. Needless to say, with the recent legalization of same-sex marriage in Massachusetts, prime time coverage of homosexuals in the media, and the spread of homosexual education in our nation's schools, America is looking more and more like Sodom and Gomorrah every day. The gay lobby is successfully changing the definition of marriage. As this definition is fundamentally redefined, other historical traditions and institutions will be looked at for redefinition as well. This will eventually change the meaning and sanctity of life, death, and birth in America and across the world.

In this modern day Sodom, gays adopt children and young people receive abortion on demand, without having to inform a parent. The church must rightfully be criticized for its slow reaction to the attack on marriage, which has been coming for quite some time. Sadly, the attack on marriage has been coming for a long time.

Today, Americans want the right to engage in whatever godless acts they deem appropriate without regard for social, moral or theological conscience. Gays wish to engage in abominable behavior without the fear of consequences. Many of them reject the idea of a God, who demands that their passions be restrained. If one dares to suggest that their lifestyle or actions are in any way wrong, either from a philosophical, theological or social standpoint, they are seen as intolerant, narrow-minded, and unenlightened.

The homosexualization of America has produced a generation that has grown up with a steady diet of television programs depicting settings tolerant of homosexuality. Such shows as *Friends*, and *Will & Grace* attempt to desensitize us to the sin of deviant sexual behavior.

Today, far too many Christians answer the gay marriage debate by saying, "What's the big deal?" Marriage, even among Christians, is not seen anymore as a sacred institution with spiritual roots. Individuals determine their own fate with disregard for moral and ethical institutions as laws are redesigned to reflect a change in the moral climate of this nation. Traditional marriage has become a casualty of the war.

Satan is using the gay community and their ideology as a weapon. He is using this weapon to tear down the fundamental institutions of society and the Church. America, a nation supposedly built on Christian principles, is being methodically broken down and replaced with a satanic system built upon sin and lies.

The homosexualization of America has produced a generation that has grown up with a steady diet of television programs depicting settings tolerant of homosexuality.

Satan is attempting to mold the world into his image and to remove all vestiges of God, godliness, and holiness. Today, people laugh at the church. They label our righteous indignation as right wing bigotry or religious fanaticism. God's people can no longer afford to be ambivalent and unconcerned about what is going on around us or about what it means.

Sodomy and homosexuality has exploded on mainstream America. It is romanticized and glamorized by the media, talk shows, politicians, and sadly by preachers and teachers of the Gospel of Jesus Christ. During President Bill Clinton's administration he endorsed a gay March on Washington that featured men dressed as women, women bare breasted, men passionately kissing other men, and open simulation of sexual perversion. These actions were just like those committed in the days of Lot, when people proudly flaunted their sin and sodomy. Gay activists became sinful soldiers, declaring war on decency, as they marched and chanted, "We're young! We're queer! We're gonna rule the world".

Books that promote homosexuality and teach our youth about homosexual sex are appearing in our elementary schools. Echoing the cry of the men of Sodom, in Genesis 19:5, Michael Swift writes in the *Gay*

Manifesto, *"We shall sodomize your sons, emblems of your feeble masculinity, we shall seduce them in your schools, in your dormitories, in your gymnasiums, in your locker rooms, in your seminaries, in your youth groups, in your movie theater bathrooms, in your army bunkhouses, in your truck stops, in your all male clubs, in your houses of Congress, wherever men are with men together. Your sons shall become our minions and do our bidding. They will be recast in our image. They will come to crave and adore us."* The Word of God says in Leviticus 18:22 on homosexuality: "Thou shalt not lie with mankind, as with womankind: it *is* abomination."

"Men and women of faith must rise up against the sweeping tide of sinful deception."

Unfortunately, the gay lobby has many Bible believing Christians afraid to stand up and speak the truth concerning the sin of homosexuality. More frightening is the fact that few seem to associate the uprising of the gay community with the last days and the return of Christ. Homosexuality is against nature and acts of homosexuality cannot produce life. As God is the creator of all, Satan wants to do nothing that gives glory to the Creator. He has strategically used the homosexual to defile men and women of every walk of life and to desecrate what should be considered holy. It is no wonder churches all over the country are filled with homosexual musicians, choir directors, pastors, preachers and teachers. It is no surprise that pedophile priests and gay bishops are the order of the day. Satan is attempting to take control of God's church and to silence the voice of those who dare oppose his abominable plan.

Men and women of faith must rise up against the sweeping tide of sinful deception. It cannot be mistaken that we are indeed living in the last days. This is underscored a thousand times when even those who are charged with upholding principles of righteousness are found advocating on behalf of accepting sinful acts. It is important to remember that sin doesn't become righteousness because the majority accepts it. Sin remains sin because it violates the law of God.

The days of Lot give us a picture of how a righteous man became so caught up in a wicked world that the angels of heaven almost had to pick him up to save him from judgment. Today, we live in a day where many refuse to take God's word seriously, much like people in Lot's day. Our days are filled with violence, murder, and abominable offences such as homosexuality, which brought about God's judgment on Sodom and Gomorrah. The social trend we are moving in will eventually lead to the judgment of God and the return of Jesus Christ our Lord. Today, we must make choices that will affect our eternal future. Jesus Christ gave up His life as a sacrifice for our sins, we should choose Him today to be Lord and Savior of our lives. As those who have boldly declared their testimonies in this book, won't you choose to be a testimony that honors God and directs your family to serve Christ? Today, won't you choose to seek God's forgiveness and prepare yourself for the return of Christ our King? If so, please repeat the following prayer:

Dear Lord, I come to you in the name of Jesus acknowledging that I am a sinner. I am sorry for my sins and the life that I have lived; Please forgive me.

I believe that your only begotten Son Jesus Christ shed His blood on the cross at Calvary and died for my sins.

Romans 10:9 says that if we confess the Lord our God and believe in our hearts that God raised Jesus from the dead, we shall be saved.

I confess Jesus as the Lord of my life. With my heart, I believe that God raised Jesus from the dead. This very moment I accept Jesus Christ as my own personal Savior and according to His Word, right now I am saved.

Thank you Jesus for your grace, which has saved me from my sins. Lord Jesus, please transform my life so that I may bring glory and honor to your name.

Amen.

"The Days of Lot" by Talbert W. Swan, II, Copyright © 2004, Used with Permission.

1/25/04 - Rev. Talbert W. Swan II, of Springfield, gives the welcoming comments to participants in the rally Mass. Voices for Traditional Marriage in the Cathedral High School auditorium in Springfield.

Afterword

Out of the Closet

By

John R. Diggs, Jr., M.D.

You have read their stories, felt their emotions, observed their experiences, and walked through their self-discovery. The history is real. The pain is palpable; the despair and hopelessness are discouraging. But at the end of the day, regeneration triumphs. All of it is here for us to see.

The power of personal testimony is genuine. There is no façade. The authors expose themselves 'warts and all.' They receive no accolades, little applause and are subject to ridicule and even attack. Truth leaps off the pages. Who could paint such unflattering portraits of themselves if they were false? The writers are so highly motivated and confident that they risk ridicule. Why would they do it? For you, that you may know that the practice of and desire for homosexual acts can be changed.

For some, to hear of overcomers gives hope, evidence that relief is not only theoretically possible but a practical reality. For others, these are warnings, that anything gay (meaning 'happy') in the homosexual lifestyle is short-lived. Following the initial elation (a phenomenon that perhaps spawned the modern application of the word "gay") a spiral ensues, inevitably downward, sometimes slowly, sometimes quickly.

Nothing scatters the darkness but light. Only truth puts lies to flight. Within these pages the truth has been revealed and the light shines forth that no one is homosexual; homosex is what some people do, not who they are.

The mere existence of these authors is proof-positive that homosexuality does not constitute an innate, unchangeable trait. Instead, it is a desperate yet destructive attempt to meet unmet developmental needs or to anesthetize emotional pain. It took years for some or the writers to realize that sexual indulgence was an ineffective way to meet those needs.

Dear reader, you have the opportunity to take advantage of the experience of others, of overcomers who now relish the truth and stand in the light rather than darkness. It is better to hear about someone who survived a fall from a high place than to experience it yourself.

From a physical point of view, the destructiveness of homosexual practice is clearly visible in the patients I have treated throughout my medical career. I was a student at the University of Buffalo School of Biomedical Sciences when the AIDS epidemic began. Of course, AIDS is not the only executioner. Some writers recount suicidal urges, others abusing their bodies with mind-numbing chemicals. A few gave us a peak into the violence that characterizes 'the lifestyle.'

All have told us of a more profound death, spiritual death. As we are all descendants of Adam, we have inherited his curse of spiritual death, a result of disobedience to God. Yet, we can be brought back to life, eternal life through the second Adam, Jesus. Just as a physically dead person does not need an alarm clock, nor does a spiritually dead person need mere awakening. The dead have need of one thing -- new life.

For most practitioners of homosexuality, it is not their homosexual activity that confirms them in spiritual death but their lack of a savior.

For sure, the abomination of homosexual sin carries with it unique penalties in the "here-and-now." First, one is cheated from understanding the order that is built into the universe. Same-sex activity contradicts the nature of humanity, which is adamantly divided into only two groups, male and female, different yet complementary. If one denies the *visible* order of humanity, one also denies the authority of the *invisible* Creator. It will then be impossible to perceive the order built into the universe, that there is a Creator, that there is an eternal destiny for each of us, and a need for the Savior. Second, one is subject to gain in the body the consequences of one's actions, disease being but one consequence of many. Lastly, the penalty of worshiping one's self (sexual same) is to be given over to vile passions by God (Romans 1). Serving one's sexual same is worshiping the creature rather the Creator.

"...relief is not only theoretically possible but a practical reality."

Let the struggles of these essayists be a 'detour sign' to those who contemplate same-sex sexual activity. May their victories be a beacon of hope to those already floundering in same-sex attraction disorder (SSAD). Allow the writers' triumphs to be an encouragement to those of us who pray for our SSAD friends, relatives, and acquaintances, to know that prayer is answered.

"And such were some of you," (1 Corinthians 6:11) says Holy Scripture as it reminds believers that the old life has no power over them. The essays in this book are living testimonies and evidence that the renewing of man (male and female) is possible.

I thank the authors for the courage of their testimonies. I thank the editor, Reverend Swan, for his willingness to endure the personal attacks in order to bring forth the truth with grace in love. And I thank God for leaving us His written word which endures when courage fades. The wise reader will not shelve this book but instead circulate it and buy another copy for someone who really needs it. You know who they are.

John R. Diggs, Jr., MD
South Hadley, MA

Rev. Talbert W. Swan, II (center), Bishop Paul S. Morton (left), Dr. William I. Shiels (right), Bishop Leroy Bailey (far right) and other black ministers condemn the comparison of gay activists efforts to legalize same-sex marriage with the civil rights movement at the U.S. Senate on May 17, 2004, the day same-sex marriage became legal in Massachusetts.

About the Authors

Pastor D.L. Foster

Pastor Darryl L. Foster is Founder and Senior Servant at Restoration Sanctuary International Church, located in metropolitan Atlanta, GA. He gladly accepted Jesus Christ as his personal Savior in April 1990 and was consequently baptized in the Holy Spirit. He was licensed to preach in 1992 by Bishop CD Owens in the Church of God in Christ while serving as associate minister at Cathedral of Prayer COGIC under Dr. Charles Rodgers. Pastor Foster served honorably for ten years with the US Army and saw combat action in the Southwest

Asia Campaign (Desert Storm). He received his secondary education at the University of Maryland and Liberty University. A seasoned writer and public speaker, Pastor Foster has ministered to thousands both nationally and internationally.

In 1996, Pastor along with Dee founded WITNESS!, the outreach ministry that has now become known worldwide for it's passion to minister to men and women trapped in unwanted homosexuality. Pastor Foster has been sought after and recognized across the country as an credible source of information and inspiration for Christian leaders who aspire to make a difference in the lives of same sex attracted people.

Pastor Foster is author of the groundbreaking book, *Touching A Dead Man: One Man's Explosive Story of Deliverance from Homosexuality* (Morris Publishing 2002). He has also freelanced with work appearing in USA Today, Charisma Magazine, the Fort Worth Star-Telegram, Ministry Today, Waco (TX) Tribune-Herald, and the Fort Benning (GA) Bayonet where he was employed as a staff writer.

John R. Diggs, Jr., M.D.

John R. Diggs Jr., MD is a board certified internist who has put his 15 years of clinical experience to work in developing a series of messages advocating the sanctity of human life and the proven benefits of sexual continence. Dr. Diggs is a tireless spokesman for "Abstinence Till Marriage." His major theme: Overwhelming scientific evidence supports the inherently reasonable and, at one time, universally held belief that sex belongs exclusively inside marriage. Dr. Diggs exposes the real-world effects of sexual permissiveness through a message that is logical, consistent, coherent and

inspiring. It leads lay persons and professionals to seek the best in themselves and their children. Parents are energized to fulfill their primary role in the education of their children. Teachers are relieved to discover their limited responsibilities in the area of sex education and their larger duty to honor the moral and ethical prerogatives of parents. Civic leaders are encouraged to find that their gut-instincts about the importance of civic virtue actually coincide with the most up-to-date findings in medicine. Businessmen learn of the costly effects of sexual immorality and   doctors have even commented that they will change their manner of practicing medicine because of the information that is presented by Dr. Diggs.

In addition to a appearing before a variety of professional conferences, churches, high school and collegiate audiences, Dr. Diggs has published numerous essays and articles for local and national print media. He has appeared on more than 100 local and national radio programs -- including the "Dr. Laura" Schlessinger show -- and television venues such as MSNBC, national Fox News and "The O'Reilly Factor."

Dr. Diggs has been married for more than a decade and is the beaming father of 3 children.

Sue Bohlin

Sue Bohlin is an associate speaker with Probe Ministries. She attended the University of Illinois, and has been a Bible teacher and Christian speaker for over twenty-five years. In addition to being a professional calligrapher, she also manages Probe's Web site. She is a Mentoring Mom for MOPS (Mothers of Pre-Schoolers), and serves on the board and as a small group leader for Living Hope Ministries, a Christ-centered outreach to thos dealing with unwanted homosexuality. She is a speaker for Christian Women's Clubs, addressing the subject "How to Handle the Things You Hate But Can't Change," based on her experience with childhood polio. Sue and her husband Ray have one son in the Air Force and another in college.

Warren Throckmorton, Ph.D.

Warren Throckmorton, Ph.D. is Director of College Counseling and an Associate Professor of Psychology at Grove City College. Professor, counselor and columnist, Dr. Throckmorton is the producer of the Truth Comes Out, a spoken word CD geared to young adults concerning sexual orientation and the I Do Exist video, a look into the lives of five former homosexuals, who answer many questions surrounding the possibility of change. His columns have been published in newspapers, magazines, and on websites across the country.

Dottie Ludwig

Dottie Ludwig in the Director of Eagles' Wings Ministry in Arden Hills, Minnesota. Eagles' Wings Ministry exists to minister to all who desire freedom from homosexuality, to support and encourage family members in their needs and desires to help their loved ones, and to educate churches and individuals that they may respond biblically, compassionately, and knowledgeably to persons who are affected by homosexuality.

Linda D. Carter

Linda Carter is the Director of Restoration Ministry of Mobile, Alabama. She attended the Nazaree Full Gospel School of Ministry, Bishop State Junior College and Alabama State University, where she majored in communications.

Linda is a former writer for the Inner City News, New Times, Inc. and Nsight Christian Publications. Linda is a strong advocate for deliverance from homosexuality and has been a guest speaker at churches, conferences, and radio stations across the country.

Alan Chambers

Alan Chambers is the President of Exodus International headquartered in Orlando, Florida. Founded in 1976, Exodus is the world's leading network dedicated to proclaiming to, educating and impacting the world with the Biblical truth that freedom from homosexuality is possible when Jesus is Lord of your life. Exodus is comprised of over 150 member and applicant agencies in North America. Having begun his successful transformation in 1990, Alan credits his own healing from homosexuality to the triadic relationship of the church, professional counseling and Exodus support group.

It is this healing combination that Exodus seeks to promote as the complete model for those pursuing change.

Alan is as a founding member of Exodus Youth and an ordained and licensed minister serving as an adjunct associate pastor on the pastoral team of Calvary Assembly, one of the largest churches in Orlando.

An accomplished speaker and writer, Alan has been published in The Orlando Sentinel, The Southern Baptist Convention's Light Magazine, Honor Bound Magazine and three award winning books: Who Moved the Goalpost: 7 Winning Strategies in Sexual Integrity Game Plan (Gresh, Moody Press 2001), 101 Frequently Asked Questions About Homosexuality (Haley, Harvest House 2004) and Saving Marriage: Putting Every Household at Risk (Staver, BH Press 2004).

Additionally, he has been featured in such media venues as: ABC's "20/20", "Nightline", MSNBC's "Buchanan and Press", "Dateline Washington", "The Alan Colmes Show", Charisma Magazine and serves as a regular guest Janet Parshall's "America".

The best part of Alan's life is sharing it with his beautiful wife, Leslie. The Chambers make their home in College Park, Florida

Tom Cole

Tom Cole is married to Donna and is the proud parent of four children, two boys and two girls. Tom and Donna openly share their freedom from homosexuality whenever given the opportunity. Tom has appeared on the national television shows 20/20, eXtra, and Inside Edition and has published his testimony and other related articles in numerous publications throughout the nation. He and his family also appeared in a television commercial promoting Exodus and ex-gay ministries. His life story is featured in Portraits of Freedom, a book published by InterVarsity Press. Tom is the Executive Director of Living Hope Ministries in Dallas, TX and is the former director of Reconciliation Ministries of Michigan.

Alan Medinger

Alan Medinger is the former Executive Director of Exodus-North America, is the founder and director of Regeneration, one of the oldest ex-gay ministries in the United States. A popular speaker for ex-gay conferences, Medinger writes a newsletter and has appeared on many shows, including The Today Show and The 700 Club.

An author, public speaker, counselor and activist, Alan has been called "one of the true sages from the Christian ex-gay movement."

From the context of his own release from homosexuality and his growth into confident and comfortable manhood, Alan offers hope to others. His landmark book, Growth Into Manhood: Resuming the Journey, offers hope for homosexually men as growth is an essential but often overlooked step in the process of healing.

Robert Winter

Robert Winter went home to be with the Lord in July 1989, shortly after his testimony was published. His words are an inspiration to many who suffer from AIDS.

Bob Ragan

Bob Ragan is the director of the Northern Virginia office of Regeneration, an Exodus referral ministry offering support for those seeking a way out of the homosexual lifestyle. Bob was actively involved with the gay community for 11 years and left it in 1987. Being full time with the ministry since January 1993, Bob provides spiritual direction, healing prayer, and coordinates support groups in the DC metro area. Bob has ministered across the US, and also in Europe, South America, and Asia. He is the vice-president of the Exodus International board of directors.

Michael Babb

Michael Babb is director of Freedom At Last in Wichita, a ministry he began in 1986. He also serves as associate pastor at Faith Community Church. Mike and his wife, Beth, have been married for 23 years and have three children.

Stephen Bennett

Stephen Bennett is a Christian Song Writer and Recording Artist whose music can be heard nationally on Christian radio. Stephen, his family and Ministry Team travel across the country sharing his music, message and incredible, life changing story. You see, Stephen *was* a homosexual, drug addict and dealer, as well as alcoholic and bulimic, until he walked away from it all in 1992. His story and music have touched the hearts of millions worldwide offering a real message of hope and love to those struggling with homosexuality.

Stephen Bennett lived the life of a homosexual until he was 28 years old. Alcoholic, bulimic and a drug addict, his destructive life style nearly killed him. Over 11 years actively as a promiscuous homosexual with countless male partners, many of Stephen's friends are now dead from AIDS. Finally, while happily involved in a long term committed relationship with a man he was in love with, Stephen was confronted by a Christian knocking at his door with a Bible in her hand. He would *never* be the same again.

Today Stephen is happily married to a beautiful Christian woman Irene who knew him when he was 'gay' and never stopped praying for him. Stephen and Irene are the parents of two beautiful little children, a boy and a girl. Their passion and commitment as a couple and as a family is to make a *difference* in the lives of millions - with *the truth*.

The Bennett's message is one of love, compassion and exhortation to the church: we need to love and reach out to the homosexual individual as Christ would. Stephen Bennett Ministries is boldly reaching out worldwide with the truth about homosexuality - and truly making a difference.

Stephen appears frequently on television and can be heard on radio. He is the Special Issues Editor on homosexuality for the American Family Association in Tupelo, MS.

Star Burch

Star Burch is from Houston, TX and currently resides in Arkansas, where she works as a military photographer. She runs an online group to help women gain knowledge and understanding on how to overcome homosexuality. Star is writing her first book and working on various other ministry projects that will help focus on change. In her own words, "I use to be a stud but now I'm a woman of God. I once was in darkness but now I have been brought into God's marvelous light!"

Mignon K. Middleton

Mignon K. Middleton is a twenty-three year old Washington, DC native. Mignon is a graduate of Duke Ellington School of the Arts and is currently studying psychology at Prince George's Community College. Mignon has been walking in deliverance from a Lesbian Identity for close to five years after embracing that identity as a teenager. She has been a committed member of the Church of the Lord's Disciple's under Pastor Deron Cloud for over four and a half years. She serves her church as an usher, a small group leader, and a member of the salvation team.

Mignon has been called by God to expose the deception involved in homosexuality and to reveal God's Word of Truth.

Jacqueline D. Carter

Jacqueline Carter resides in Atlanta, GA and is a member of Restoration Sanctuary International Church under the leadership of Pastor D.L. Foster.

Ron Elmore

Ron Elmore is the Director of *Beyond Imagination Ministries*, a ministry that exists to bring God's healing and redemptive power to those who struggle with homosexuality and other sexual addictions. By coming along side those who struggle--offering them love, compassion, encouragement, exhortation and an understanding of the issues—it is the hope of Ron and his staff that the struggler will grow spiritually, emotionally and mentally.

Ron believes that "homosexuality is a manifestation of a wounded life and works to "heal" homosexuals from the gay lifestyle.

Donald L. Johnson

Minister Donald L. Johnson received the baptism of the Holy Ghost at a Deliverance Service at the Bible Church of Christ, Mount Vernon, New York in 1987. He surrendered his life to the Lord, Jesus Christ in January,1989. After his surrender, he immediately joined the church founded by Bishop Dr. Roy Bryant, Senior who is also the Pastor. Shortly thereafter, Minister Johnson joined the Gospel Chorus and later served as its President. He has studied extensively under his pastor's tutelage and Minister Johnson was ordained a minister of the gospel of Jesus Christ in 1996.

Donald volunteers as a Protestant chaplain at several correctional facilities throughout New York and is employed by Westchester County Government as a Probation Officer. He holds a Bachelor of Science degree in Human and Community Services and a Masters in Public Administration from Marist College in Poughkeepsie, N.Y.

169

Stephanie Boston

Stephanie D. Boston is the ministry facilitator of Restoration @ St.James A.M.E. Church, located in Newark, NJ. under Senior Pastor, Rev. William D. Watley, Ph.D. She was raised in the A.M.E. church by her grandmother and accepted Jesus Christ as her personal Savior at age 10. Her relationship with Christ was restored in February of 2000. Since that time she has continued to grow

for God's glory. In March of 2003, Stephanie was given permission to start a deliverance ministry for those who struggle with homosexuality. Under the guidance of her pastor and executive minister who through a Visions' Conference encouraged the church to provide seven star service to the needs of the congregation. On February 10, 2004 the ministry was birthed.

Mike Haley

Mike Haley is a member of the Public Policy division of Focus on the Family in Colorado Springs, CO and helped to develop the Love Won Out conference. He is a frequent speaker at conferences nationwide and has written articles for publications such as, *Single Parent and Plugged In*. He has recently produced the newest booklet for Focus called *Straight Answers: Exposing the Myths and Facts about Homosexuality*. Mike's testimony of change from homosexuality appears on several documentary videos including *Reaching into the Closet* and *A Journey Out*.

He and his wife, Angie, were married in 1994 and are the proud parents of two young sons.

Kevin D. Giles

Kevin Giles is a native of Los Angeles, CA. He currently resides in a suburban area of the city with his family. Kevin is the author of *Gay, But Not Happy: Dealing With Your Unwanted Homosexuality*. He has been free from the homosexual lifestyle for 12 years.

Kevin is a trained marriage mentor and attends Faithful Central Bible Church in Inglewood, CA under the leadership of Bishop Kenneth Ulmer. Kevin holds a Bachelor of Science from Biola University.

Steve Rooks

Steve Rooks was a principle dancer for the Martha Graham Dance Company from 1981-1991. His performance credits with the Graham Company include the Metropolitan Opera House presentation of *Diversion of Angels* televised for "Celebrate! 100 Years of the Lively Arts at the Met", and as a featured dancer on the television special, "The Martha Graham Company in Japan".

Mr Rooks' choreographic credits include a solo--*Outside*, which was selected to be presented in the 1989 New Choreographers series during the Graham Company's fall season at City Center Theater in New York. A later work--*Cool River*, became a part if that company's 1996-1997 repertoire after its World Premier at Lincoln Center. Mr. Rooks currently serves as resident choreographer for the Vassar Repertory Dance Theatre.

Besides his work as assistant professor of dance at Vassar, Mr. Rooks is also a regular guest instructor at the Alvin Ailey and Martha Graham Schools of Dance. He has also taught internationally at several dance festivals, as well as the Dallsa Black Dance Theater, Ballet Nacional de Mexico, The American Academy of Ballet, and the Houston Ballet.

Bummi Niyonu Anderson

Bummi Anderson is a member of Restoration Sanctuary Church in College Park, GA. She is the author of Out of Darkness into His Marvelous Light, a book in which she bears her soul in sharing her experience as a lesbian. It is a heart moving novel of triumph over the homosexual lifestyle.

Active in ministry, Bummi is a graduate of Albany State University.

Vanessa Jaudon

Vanessa resides in Atlanta, GA, where she engages in ministry full-time. She also manages various gospel artists and groups. Through seeking God, Vanessa was delivered from lesbianism. She stands on Matthew 6:33 in all that she does, *"Seek ye first the Kingdom of God, and all His righteousness, and all these things shall be added unto you."*

Talbert W. Swan, II

Rev. Talbert W. Swan, II, an ordained minister with credentials from the Church of God in Christ, has served as a Pastor, Associate Pastor, Youth Pastor and Bible teacher. He now ministers at various congregations throughout the United States. Rev. Swan currently serves as the pastor of the Solid Rock Church of God in Christ in Indian Orchard, MA. He serves on the Jurisdictional level as Executive Secretary to the Jurisdictional Bishop of the Greater Massachusetts Jurisdiction.

Rev. Swan has been at the forefront of church and community activities, especially in the area of social justice and racial reconciliation. He is the co-founder of the Springfield Christian Leadership Council, and ecumenical group of pastors and lay leaders committed to eradicating racism within the Christian church. Pastor Swan has served as an executive board member to the National Association for the Advancement of Colored People, delegate to the State of Massachusetts Democratic Convention, an advisor to the Mayor of Springfield, and member of the Springfield Human Relations Commission. He current serves as a board member on the Indian Orchard Main Street Partnership, member of the Hartford Seminary Alumni/ae Council, member of the Harvard Divinity School Black Alumni/ae Council, and the National Chaplain of the Iota Phi Theta Fraternity, Inc. Pastor Swan also serves the National Church of God in Christ as a member of the Executive Committee of the General Assembly, an Executive Board Member of the General Council of Pastors and Elders, and a Special Assistant to the General Secretary.

Pastor Swan's writings include columns and editorials for various newspapers. He is the author of several books, including: *"Addressing Violence in Springfield Schools: Why Springfield Cannot Allow the Death of Rev. Theodore N. Brown to be in Vain"* (ISBN 0-9716355-0-1), and *"No More Cursing: Destroying the Roots of Religious Racism"* (ISBN 0-9716355-1-x).

Pastor Swan holds an Associate in Science, a Bachelor of Science in Religious Studies, and a Master of Arts in Theology degree. He is a graduate of Hartford Seminary and Harvard Divinity School.

Rev. Talbert W. Swan, II speaks with reporters on May 17, 2004 after a press conference at the U.S. Senate in Washington D.C. where black ministers condemned the legalization of same-sex marriage and its comparison with the civil rights movement.

Resources

Books

Out of Darkness Into His Marvelous Light
by Bummi Niyonu Anderson
ISBN 0-9715323-7-0

Touching A Dead Man: One Man's Explosive Story of Deliverance from Homosexuality
by DL Foster
ISBN 0-9723510-0-0

Gay But Not Happy
by Kevin Giles
ISBN 0-9721760-0-4

Escaping the Gay Lifestyle: Confirmation of a Divine Call
by Evangelist Miriam Passmore

Growth into Manhood: Resuming the Journey
by Alan P. Medinger
ISBN 0-8778830-6-8

The Truth Comes Out Leader's Guide
by Warren Throckmorton
0-9746706-1-8

Let No Man Put Asunder: A Biblical Perspective on Marriage
By Talbert W. Swan, II
0-9716355-3-3

Straight Answers: Exposing the Myths and Facts About Homosexuality
by Mike Haley

Internet

Exodus International
http://www.exodus-international.org

Witness Ministries
www.witnessfortheworld.org

Stephen Bennett Ministries
www.SBMinistries.org

Dr. Warren Throckmorton
www.drthrockmorton.com

National Association for Research and Therapy of Homosexuality (NARTH)
www.narth.com

HOPE Ministries
www.homosexresolve.netministries.org

International Healing Foundation
www.gaytostraight.org

Parents and Friends of Ex=Gays and Gays
www.pfox.org

Probe Ministries
www.probe.org

Beyond Imagination
www.beyondimagination.org

Restoration Ministry of Mobile
www.expage.com/restorationministrymobile

Eagle's Wings Ministry
www.ewm.org

Freedom At Last
www.freedomatlast.org

Living Hope Ministries
www.livehope.org

Shattering Illusions
www.shattering-illusions.com

Solid Rock Church of God in Christ
www.srcogic.com

Made in the USA
Lexington, KY
23 April 2011